BOBBY AND CAROLYN

A Memoir of My Two Mothers

Also by John Philip Drury

POETRY
The Teller's Cage: Poems and Imaginary Movies (2024)
Sea Level Rising (2015)
The Refugee Camp (2011)
Burning the Aspern Papers (2003)
The Disappearing Town (2000)
The Stray Ghost (1987)

BOOKS ABOUT POETRY
The Poetry Dictionary (2006, 1995)
Creating Poetry (1991)

BOBBY AND CAROLYN

A Memoir of My Two Mothers

Also by John Philip Drury

POETRY
The Teller's Cage: Poems and Imaginary Movies (2024)
Sea Level Rising (2015)
The Refugee Camp (2011)
Burning the Aspern Papers (2003)
The Disappearing Town (2000)
The Stray Ghost (1987)

BOOKS ABOUT POETRY
The Poetry Dictionary (2006, 1995)
Creating Poetry (1991)

BOBBY AND CAROLYN

A Memoir of My Two Mothers

by

John Philip Drury

Finishing Line Press
Georgetown, Kentucky

Copyright © 2024 by John Philip Drury
ISBN 979-8-88838-597-5 First Edition
All rights reserved under International and Pan-American Copyright Conventions. No part of this book may be reproduced in any manner whatsoever without written permission from the publisher, except in the case of brief quotations embodied in critical articles and reviews.

Publisher: Leah Huete de Maines
Editor: Christen Kincaid
Cover Art: Family snapshot taken in December 1958
Author Photo: Tess Despres Weinberg
Cover Design: Elizabeth Maines McCleavy

Order online: www.finishinglinepress.com
also available on amazon.com

Author inquiries and mail orders:
Finishing Line Press
PO Box 1626
Georgetown, Kentucky 40324
USA

Contents

The House That She Designed 1
Disclosure #1 4
Return of the Lyric Soprano 5
Disclosure #2 8
Fishing Pier and Hunting Lodge 9
Disclosure #3 11
Labor Day 12
Disclosure #4 16
My Mother's Choice 17
Disclosure #5 31
Broken Music 32
Disclosure #6 38
Separate Residences 39
Disclosure #7 43
Aria in the State Mental Hospital 44
Disclosure #8 57
Beautiful Bobby from Downtown Bethesda 59
Disclosure #9 64
Why I Went to Summer Camp 65
Disclosure #10 69
Domestic Arrangements 70
Disclosure #11 74
Night Rumblings on Massachusetts Avenue 75
Disclosure #12 79
Breaking Up and Getting Back Together 80
Disclosure #13 83
Prodigal Son in the Army 84
Disclosure #14 89

Keeping a Schedule 90
Disclosure #15 93
Three-Bedroom Apartment 96
Disclosure #16 103
Vissi d'arte, vissi d'amore 105
Disclosure #17 109
Exile in Cincinnati 110
Disclosure #18 113
Give All to Love 114
Disclosure #19 116
What Really Happened 117
Disclosure #20 120
The Arms of Morpheus 122
Disclosure #21 128
Making Lists 129
Disclosure #22 133
Varieties of Religious Experience 134
Disclosure #23 140
Full Moon on the Water 142

Acknowledgments 149

In memory of
Carolyn Bayly Drury
and
Carolyn Creighton Long

Vittoria, vittoria, mio core!

two women together is a work
nothing in civilization has made simple

    —Adrienne Rich, "Twenty-One Love Poems" (XIX)

The House That She Designed

My mother stood at the top of the attic stairs, on the brink of a choice she would have to make. If she had looked out the window behind her, she could have seen the spite fence that Aunt Carrie had installed, the acres of boxwood behind it, and the Christ Church cemetery where her father and older sister and so many of her ancestors were buried. She could have gazed at her own back yard, the lovely twisting trunks of crepe myrtles, the drooping green hammock, the upside-down wading pool, the swing set with its sliding board, the tool shed at one corner and the log-cabin playhouse at the other. She could have seen, just over the low fence that bordered the adjacent yard, the remains of her father's rock garden, the spot where she saw him swallow pills from a bottle on the day he died in 1933.

She had grown up in the sprawling house next door. When she and her husband, Phil, moved back to her hometown on the Eastern Shore of Maryland, mainly because she was homesick, she paid her mother for this parcel of land that used to be part of the side yard of the big house. When she met with the contractor, she drew a plan of the house she wanted. There had to be a screen porch, but it was an integral part of the structure, tucked in like a room on the right corner. From the porch, a door with a brass knocker led to a small living room with a fireplace. An arched opening led to the dining room and beyond that to a kitchen big enough for a round table with a checkered oilcloth where she could enjoy breakfast. There were two bedrooms on the ground floor, with a bathroom in between. At the back door, there was a utility room with a wringer washing machine. There was no basement, but at the center of the ground floor there was a large grate over the gravity furnace that warmed the whole house but never really worked to her satisfaction.

Upstairs from the grate was the attic, where she stood and looked down. Around her was the playroom I had claimed as my bedroom, with a Lionel train layout and bins of toys. Recently, I had started sleeping downstairs again, and she had just removed the pictures taped to the slanting ceiling above my attic bed: a gallery of rock-and-roll singers, which I had placed there in imitation of the bedroom walls decorated by the neighborhood's teenaged girls who liked to play Top 40 music on their transistor radios, who took turns babysitting, walking me to Long Wharf where we visited the cook in the galley of the *Potomac*, the former presidential yacht that would eventually be owned by Elvis Presley. Because I had crushes on those much-older girls, I cut out photographs and applied them to the ceiling, like a junior version of Michelangelo on his back in the Sistine Chapel. My mother felt no compunctions about removing this collage dedicated to puppy love. The

1

grocery bag stuffed with crumpled pictures lay on its side next to where she stood at the top of the stairs.

She had designed her own house, but since she wasn't an architect, it looked like a simplified house in a child's drawing, no more than a cottage, the shape of a small milk carton, four white walls and a green-shingled roof. "It cost $8,000," she told me, "like every other house I ever owned." She and my father had bought their first house in Secane, Pennsylvania, when he was finishing college at Swarthmore after his discharge from active duty in the army. He had also worked two jobs there while she stayed at home and tried to figure out how to be a housewife. They bought and sold the house for $8,000. She never made any profits on her investments.

Now her husband was gone. She had a son to care for, and a woman instead of a man in her life. She was sure that everyone in town was gossiping about her. Separation was bad enough. Divorce was uncommon and shameful. Her mother, Sadie, was asking questions and impatient about getting no satisfactory answers. She didn't have a job, since my father had been the money earner in the family, working as a teller at the National Bank of Cambridge. Her contributions had been her dwindling inheritance, her valuable antiques, and her connections that landed him the job in the first place. Now he was gone, living in a one-room apartment in lower Manhattan. I was at school. Her friend Carolyn, the soprano who had suffered a nervous breakdown in Italy and had returned home to a rapturous welcome, but no more rapturous than here in the little house my mother had designed, was out and about who knew where, doing who knew what.

Houses are meant to protect, but they also restrain, keep the wild forces contained and under control. They seal, smother, stifle, cramp, and contort when the fit is too tight. My mother didn't know what to do, where to go, whom she could talk to, how she could clean up the mess in this tidy dwelling. With the site of her father's rock garden out the window behind her, she threw herself down the stairs.

How, exactly, can anyone throw herself? I imagine her diving headfirst, like someone at the edge of the pool but without aiming her arms ahead like a prow to open up the water. She started tumbling, banging into the walls of the cramped passageway, Eurydice gladly descending to hell the fast way, hitting each wall, back and forth, and skipping some of the steps, banging her elbows and knees, hurting her back and her butt and her hair, aware as she fell that the kerchief she tied on her head to clean the attic room had fallen around her neck, worried that she might be strangled by silk as she bounded toward the heating grate in the floor below, rumbling like a sack of laundry down a chute, thinking *Stupid, how stupid, you stupid girl!* as her arms and legs scraped the door frame at the bottom and her body settled in a crumpled heap.

She heard the rumbling drone of the gravity furnace and felt very hot on one side and very cold on the other. It was the middle of autumn, so the heat had flicked on, but the windows downstairs were wide open. She heard the bells of the Catholic church begin ringing and the dogs of the neighborhood howling along. That she was still alive was anticlimactic.

Eventually, she started to worry that someone would come into the house and discover her contorted, injured body on the floor. *Don't let it be Carolyn*, she thought, *and not Mother*. Anyone could have entered the cramped house, because she never locked the front door. *Don't, oh God no, don't let it be Johnny*, she thought as she tried to get up.

It was hard, and it hurt, but she managed to get on her knees, which had both undergone operations to remove cartilage. *My football knees*, she thought, smiling a little and then noticing she was smiling. Life wasn't good, but it had its attractions and attachments, and it wasn't so easy to dispose of.

She looked up the attic stairs and finally noticed the window at the top. Then she started to cry. She knew she had to do something. Leave Carolyn. Leave Cambridge. The only thing she absolutely had to hold onto was her son.

She leaned to the right, making the transition from kneeling to sitting, and checked herself for injuries, amazed that nothing seemed to be broken. She rubbed her hands down arms and legs, around her face and neck, but didn't feel any cuts, no blood coming up on her palms or fingers. She hurt like hell and knew there would be bruises to deal with and to explain, but an intentional fall could become an accident after the fact. God wouldn't like what she had done. So what was she going to do now? She was worried about internal bleeding, but she didn't want to go to the hospital. She got up and found that her knees didn't give, didn't buckle, didn't seize up. The people she loved would return home soon. She could lie down on her tester bed, or turn on the television and sit on the living-room sofa, or go to the bathroom and pee, or go to the kitchen and brew some coffee in the percolator. It was the middle of the day, too early to start drinking, but that was the one thing she needed, one of her "sody pops," so she cracked open some ice from the ice box, dropped it into a glass tumbler, and poured in a jigger of bourbon and some Coca-Cola. She leaned back against the counter, aching all over but alive in her shaken nerves, and knew one thing. She had to sell the house. She had to leave. And she wouldn't tell anyone about her fall, how she threw herself down the attic steps, trying to kill herself, until she was in hospice care in a nursing home. It was one more secret she would keep as long as she could.

Disclosure #1

My mother used to say she would come back and haunt me if I ever joined a jacket club (like a juvenile delinquent in a motorcycle gang) or became a ballet dancer (worrying about my erotic development, even though I wasn't graceful enough for pliés, relevés, and sautés) or wrote this memoir about her. And that's what she's done, haunting me like a muse.

She didn't talk about throwing herself downstairs, trying to kill herself, until a few weeks before she died. I'm not sure she ever told anyone else. She left it to me to flesh out the scene, and that's what I've done in this opening chapter of a memoir that is both hers and mine. I know the scene intimately because it took place in my bedroom in the attic of a small house where I lived for the first eight-and-a-half years of my life. I still hear the stories she told and retold, the phrases and sentences and cadences of her voice. I still hear her maxims, jokes, and warnings. I'm her medium in an ongoing séance.

Her given name was Carolyn, the same as the "glamorous soprano," Carolyn Long, who entered our lives in 1956 and never left. It could have been confusing, except that my mother's nickname was Bobby. "I was supposed to be a boy," she told me. "Shep and Sadie were both in their forties when I was born, and he desperately wanted a son. Everyone at the hospital knew it, and they didn't want to disappoint him, so when I was born, a nurse came out to the waiting room and announced, 'Little Bobby is here!' And wouldn't you know it? The name stuck."

Her father owned a dry goods store on Race Street. He was overly sensitive, a gentle man who could "dish it out," meaning tease other people, but "couldn't take it." In 1933, when she was nine, his store caught fire and his sisters burned the will that left him the finest house on High Street.

That was the summer when she saw him standing in his rock garden, next to the rose arbor and wrought-iron bench. "What are you doing, Daddy?" she called, but he didn't answer. Sometimes she remembered watching him from her bedroom window. Other times, she remembered following him out to the garden. "Daddy took some sleeping pills," she told me, "and they upset his stomach. The doctor pumped them out, but he died from internal bleeding." It's no coincidence that she claimed she couldn't remember anything that happened before she was nine years old, when she saw her father kill himself.

Return of the Lyric Soprano

"I heard some big news today," my father announced at the dinner table. "Carolyn Long is coming back to Cambridge."

"Who's that?" I said. I was almost six years old, obsessed with Mickey Mantle, Elvis Presley, and Roy Rogers.

"She's a famous opera singer, and she's coming back from Italy," my father said.

"She had a nervous breakdown," my mother added, "or at least that's what I heard. Her father's Captain Amos, who lives on Water Street."

"What's an opera?" I asked. "What's a nervous breakdown?"

I learned that operas are plays that are sung instead of spoken. It reminded me of our kindergarten show in which I played the Muffin Man ("who lives on Drury Lane") and sang the song, wearing an apron and a chef's hat while a package of Hostess Twinkies slid back and forth on the round tray I held.

I learned that nervous breakdowns require rest and that Carolyn Long would have to relax and take it easy for a while before she could return to the stage and resume her singing career. In the meantime, my father saw an opportunity: "Maybe I can study voice with her." He was already outgrowing his role as tenor in the Christ Church choir. He had performed solos during services and at variety shows the church put on. He had sung on the local radio station that was located on a spit of land that jutted out on the Choptank River. He had caught the singing bug. He knew he needed voice lessons from a professional singer, and his chance had arrived in the form of a prodigal daughter who was coming home to recuperate.

My father met her to talk about taking lessons. "She had me sing a couple of scales, starting on a pitch that was comfortable for me"—he demonstrated with a sustained *ah* that went up several notes and down again—"then she stopped me and said, *You're really a baritone, Phil, but if you're trained properly you can sing tenor roles. Caruso did that. Taught himself how to negotiate a high C. But you're not producing it from your diaphragm, down here. It's coming through your nose, so it sounds like a kazoo. When can we start?*"

Dad was gaga about his new voice teacher. He showed us the promotional flyer she gave him, with a close-up on one side and a sexy photo of her leaning slinkily against a wall, a curly-haired brunette seething toward the camera, on the reverse. Under her name, it said "Glamorous Soprano." There were raves from critics too, but I didn't read those then.

I met Carolyn when her parents, Captain Amos and Nellie Creighton, gave a lawn party to welcome her back home in the yard that ran down to the bulwark and little strip of beach by the Choptank River. Since Amos was a waterman, once the commander of the Maryland Oyster Fleet, his house was decorated with nautical artifacts. The back staircase was a ship's ladder that you were supposed to climb down backwards, holding both railings, not forward as on a regular set of steps. There was a ship's life preserver on the wall and some portholes. Inside, on the floor of his kitchen, stood a large brass binnacle.

The first thing I remember about Carolyn is when she boomed, on the windy lawn by the river, "You children have got to behave! Now line up right here for inspection. I'm the sergeant major, and I want to make sure you all pass muster." Coastal warning pennants fluttered from a mast in Captain Amos's yard.

All of the kids had been running around, and now I felt a little frightened, standing at attention beside my cousin Dail (who was always Dale Evans to my Roy Rogers when we played cowboy), lined up in a row with the other boys and girls. She was holding a fife because she had just come from the practice of a fife and drum corps she belonged to. When Carolyn reached her, she smiled, reached out to stroke her short brown hair, and said, "Darling, you must play me an air on that little flute. Pronto." Dail raised her fife and tooted out the opening bars of "Yankee Doodle."

"Oh my, what a dreadful song," Carolyn said, "but you played it beautifully, my dearest one. You're Dorothy's daughter, aren't you?" She was.

"And you, you handsome boy," she said, turning her radiant brown eyes upon me, "you must be Phil and Bobby's son. Marvelous to make your acquaintance." She rubbed my short bristle of hair and said, "That's for luck and long life." Then she moved down the formation, continuing her inspection of the ragtag troops.

I was smitten, but not everyone liked her. One blustery afternoon, when my mother and Carolyn drove to Oxford, a charming town on the Tred Avon River, they let me bring along my friend Jack, who was a real baby, still sucking milk from a bottle at the age of five. It was cold enough for jackets, and the river was kicking up white-caps as we watched the ferry moving off toward Bellevue on the distant shore.

Carolyn stood on the pier, legs apart like an old sea captain—she was wearing trousers—and took deep breaths of the wind that was surging and making our jackets billow and flap.

"Isn't it dramatic, my darlings?" she asked us. "You feel truly alive when a gale is blowing."

"I want to go back to the car," Jack whined.

"Why, then, go back, go back! Don't be a jackass."

Jack ran back to the car, where my mother was already sitting, smoking a cigarette. Later, still mad, he called me a "Johnny ass." He had never heard the expression and thought that Carolyn was singling out his name to make fun of him.

She liked to cook and offered me home-made cupcakes and Jell-O with chunks of fresh fruit inside. She introduced me to salmon for breakfast, and real spaghetti with clam sauce, instead of what I was used to (gobs of pasta and meatballs from a can), for late-night dinners. She called herself "the old feed bag."

Carolyn and my mother would return to Oxford many times by themselves. Margaret Carreau, a pianist and composer, lived in a house overlooking the wide river, and they were frequent guests. Carolyn had performed Margaret's published art songs in her concerts, and the two of them were almost certainly practicing new ones, in the hope that she could revive her performing career and tour again, as well as enjoying martinis on the screen porch. On one trip, Carolyn and my mother were standing on a pier by the ferry landing and my mother suddenly jumped into the water with all her clothes on. She may have wanted to show Carolyn that there was nothing to be afraid of, since her friend couldn't swim, even though she had grown up on the water, sailing, fishing, and helping her father, Captain Amos, tong for oysters. She may have wanted to prove to Carolyn that she would do anything for her, anything. She may have been angry, or hurt, or happy, or drunk. All I know is that, on a day when I was somewhere else, my mother jumped into the cold shallow water.

Disclosure #2

My mother was supposed to be a boy, and I was supposed to be a girl named Elizabeth, after her beloved older sister who was killed by a Victor Lynn truck at a crossroads in Delaware when she was wearing sunglasses and couldn't see the vehicle bearing down from her left as she accelerated across the highway. "They asked me what to call you," my mother told me, "and I said, 'Take him back! I ordered a girl.' I didn't have a boy's name picked out because I knew you were going to be a girl. And the nurse said, 'But we have to write down something on the birth certificate.' And I said, 'Call him John!'"

"I always liked the name John," my father explained when I asked him about it. "Of course we decided on it in advance. That's silly." His uncle, a choir director, was also named John, so it counted as a family name.

My parents often had conflicting memories of experiences they had shared. They disagreed, for example, about what happened when I was born. My mother claimed that she was in labor for days. "It was a difficult delivery," she said. "I almost died! The doctor asked your father, 'It's her or the baby. Who should we save?' And he said, 'The mother.' The doctor told me I wouldn't be able to have any more children. It was too dangerous. And I didn't." That was her explanation of why I was an only child.

My father, however, dismissed her version, saying, "She had an easy delivery." It made my mother furious when I reported his words back to her. "I wish men could get pregnant," she said, fuming. "That would be the last baby ever born."

Fishing Pier and Hunting Lodge

An old man in hip boots stands in shallow water, just before it merges into the Chesapeake Bay, reeling in his fishing line and then casting again, re-baiting as the need arises with chunks of peeler crab he keeps in a pocket. He's catching rockfish, the Maryland term for striped bass. He looks old, but he will get much older and toward the end of his life will build his own sailboat and sail alone on the bay. He looks at home standing in the water but does not know how to swim. Like other watermen, his skills involve staying afloat, keeping his vessel from capsizing, tonging for oysters and pulling up crab traps. He served for fifty years as commander of the Maryland Oyster Fleet, which means that above all else he's a politician. He's wearing a floppy hat because it's sunny, but wind has started blowing, so he's tied the hat under his bristly chin.

His daughter, the opera singer, has inherited his beautiful curls. Her press releases claim he's a singer too, but his performances usually take place at night, on a boat or in the yacht club, when he's drinking and belts out "Old Man River." She's given up touring for the time being and is wading in the bay, tentative in her black swimsuit that shows off her buxom figure. She's learning how to swim. My mother, wearing a bathing cap and a frilly pink swimsuit, is teaching her to stroke and kick, encouraging her to relax while she cradles her in her arms.

My father, a skinny veteran who wants to be a singer, is fishing on a rickety, zig-zag pier, but unlike Captain Amos he's not catching anything. He's singing, but the wind is picking up strength and I can't hear the words, although it sounds like a straining attempt at an aria.

I'm sitting by myself about halfway down the pier, wishing I could swim but prohibited because of the ointment and bandage on the back of my right knee where a spider bit me. At least that's how the two Carolyns—the singer and my mother—have diagnosed the oozing pustule, which looks like a miniature volcano.

The scene has taken on a glow, like a picture in a tiny shrine, lit by a votive candle. My wife would call it a "flashbulb memory." It reminds me of Proust, how tripping over the uneven paving stones in the Baptistery of San Marco recalls a similar stumble in Combray. Wind invokes Wingate, a spit of uneasy land across from Lower Hooper's Island, which is uninhabited. I gaze at a group portrait: Captain Amos, my mother, my father, and the "glamorous soprano" who's come between my parents.

The wind accelerates, and clouds that appeared like a mountain range over a long, flat island and the wide bay have nearly reached us, lightning hitting the water and thunder grumbling. We retreat to a hunting lodge by the pier, where a caretaker latches the shutters and locks the door. We're all afraid, except for Captain Amos, as rain tattoos the tin roof and wind rattles the shutters and whines under the doors and down the chimney into the big fireplace where the caretaker lights tinder for a fire, even though it's August.

The funny thing is, I don't remember the storm passing, or trotting out to the Chevrolet as the last drops of rain peter out. The windy, sunny day on the edge of the water always ends with a summer squall that traps us in the hunting lodge, like characters in Sartre's *No Exit*. It's the last time we find ourselves together in one room, a temporary refuge from the permanent storm, so I hold on and won't let the light blow out.

Disclosure #3

I have never returned to the location of the most intense memory of my childhood. The lodge is probably long gone. But I wrote a poem about the experience over a decade before I began working on this memoir, a pantoum with a title that I knew was inaccurate, "Storm on Fishing Bay." Composing the previous chapter allowed me to flesh out details, but the song-like qualities inherent in the repeating, circular Malay poetic form do underscore the musical interests of the main characters. Now that the poem is being reprinted, I'm giving it a new title, "Storm Approaching":

> What's hard to explain
> darkens the prospect of happiness—
> like wind picking up off shore
> where four people retreat separately.
>
> Darkened, the prospect of happiness
> falls back to a hunting lodge
> where four people retreat, separately
> latching shutters, brewing coffee, gazing.
>
> Fall's back. In a hunting lodge,
> who is stirring the dust—
> latching shutters, brewing coffee, gazing
> at pictures spilled from an album?
>
> Who is not stirring the dust?
> The mother fussing? The boy who ponders
> pictures spilled from an album?
> The father quiet? The beautiful stranger singing?
>
> The mother fusses at her boy, who ponders
> what's hard to explain:
> the father quiet, the beautiful stranger singing
> like wind picking up off shore.

Labor Day

Labor Day Weekend came and went in 1958, and so did my father, who took the Chevy Bel-Air and left home in the middle of the night. He left no note telling my mother where he was going. He didn't give notice at the National Bank. He didn't tell any of his friends who bowled with him, or played bridge, or golfed at the country club. My mother must have been out of her mind with worry, but she never betrayed any of that to me. School was starting, so she made me a breakfast of hard-boiled egg and scrapple and shooed me off to walk to the Academy School, less than half a block away. My father may have gone to whereabouts unknown, but my mother acted as though nothing had changed, so the days after he abandoned us proceeded as usual.

My mother had a gift for covering up her fears when it mattered—which means when it came to protecting her only child. Thunder had always terrified her. When she was growing up in the big house next door, she cowered in her bedroom with the shades drawn and a pillow pulled over her head to muffle the rumbling. Sadie and Sarah (her mother and the grown-up sister she disliked) would sit on rocking chairs on the screen porch and watch the regatta of dark clouds, the lightning strikes on the river, and listen to thunder reverberating as if it came from bass drums in a Loyalty Day parade. They'd enjoy the stiff breezes, along with stiff drinks in highball glasses, after a hot day. Once, when I was little, we were caught in a hurricane on the Choptank River and had to ride it out aboard a cabin cruiser. My mother was sure the boat was going to capsize and we were all going to drown, but she never let on how much thunderstorms scared her.

And she never acted scared about the thunderstorm that her own life had become. Soon enough, though, she had to let me know that something was different. My father wasn't joining us at breakfast or dinner, but Carolyn was usually present, there at night when I went to bed, even tucking me in, and there when I woke up in the morning, offering me hot dogs or green peas or Bundt cake or apple pie or salt mackerel for breakfast. When my mother left to meet my father at Wilmington so he could return the car and the keys and take a train back to New York, she had to explain why the automobile was back but my father was not.

"Johnny," she began, "your daddy's living in New York City now. He wants to find a better job and he wants to be a singer. You'll visit him soon." She hugged me and then added, "He likes to ride the subways."

"What are subways?" I asked.

"Well, they're trains that go underground, below the streets, through the tunnels. Maybe we'll join him someday, and you can ride the subway too."

Many of the pupils in Mrs. Johnson's third-grade class used their show-and-tell time to tell us about trips they had taken with their families. The most popular destination was Hershey, Pennsylvania, to tour the chocolate factory. The best part was when a classmate shared a big bag of Hershey kisses or a box of Hershey bars. As the fall went on, I wondered how my report on New York would go over when I finally visited my father.

It was cold when the Trailways bus arrived at Port Authority terminal in Manhattan and my father met me. We descended to the subway station, and I was thrilled to be riding a train through an endless tunnel, especially since the bus had made me sick to my stomach. I liked the whooshing and clattering sounds the subway made and the way brightly lit stations emerged from the darkness. I was fascinated by the leather straps people held as they stood and swayed.

My father lived just north of Greenwich Village on 16th Street, in an apartment we reached by climbing up several flights. The stairwell was dimly lit, the wall-paper dingy, slightly tattered, and the carpet worn, some of the dark reds of the diagonal patterns showing through to scuffed floorboards. When I put my hand on the brown wooden railing, my father said, "Don't touch it. It's dirty."

His apartment consisted of a single room with a kitchenette, a couch, a daybed, a couple of lumpy chairs, some tables with lamps, and an oval braided rug. The small bathroom had a toilet but no bath. "It's next to the kitchen sink," he laughed, and opened two cabinet doors under the counter to show me the tub. "You pull up the countertop—see how it's divided in sections?—and prop it up under the cupboard. Presto. It's easy."

We stayed there as little as possible. He took me to Rockefeller Center to see the ice skaters, and we stood at a railing above the rink that radiated coolness. We didn't skate ourselves. Neither of us knew how, although I liked roller-skating at the Arena rink in Cambridge. As we walked around the Art Deco buildings, I was impressed by a statue of Atlas holding up a hollow world that looked as though it was made of hoops. We walked down Fifth Avenue and rode an elevator up to the observation deck of the Empire State Building. We rode a subway down to the Battery and took the Staten Island Ferry across and back. The best thing we did, though, was visit Times Square, where I loved the wide waterfall that was part of a Pepsi-Cola advertisement on top of one building, which wasn't very tall, and the Camel billboard where puffs of smoke emerged from the open mouth of a smoker's painted face. The glitter of flashing neon signs was thrilling, and the Ripley's Believe-It-Or-Not Museum was fun, especially seeing the Iron Maiden and being horrified by the spikes on the inside of that body-shaped torture chamber.

We ate lunch in a diner on Sixth Avenue called the Hamburger Train. Three-rail toy tracks ran along the counter, right behind the napkin dispensers and the salt and pepper shakers. I heard the toot of a whistle and saw puffs of smoke rising. Plates of hamburgers and French fries arrived on flat cars pulled by a Lionel steam locomotive marked for the New York Central. We picked our orders off the cars ourselves, and then the train started up again and made its way around the loop into the kitchen.

My father was showing me why he couldn't resist New York. He never said a word about what he had done, why he had left home, or when my mother and I might be moving there. I knew he was working as a bank teller and singing in the choir at St. Bartholomew's Church on Park Avenue. I knew he was finally being paid for his singing.

Near the end of my visit, I left one of my gloves on the subway. He looked hurt, pursing his lips, as though I had done it on purpose, but he didn't scold me that time. I would lose a number of gloves and scarves during future trips to Manhattan. "You're always forgetting something!" he would say. It became a catch phrase, but I think I was leaving a kind of trail, unconsciously letting him know that part of me would remain in the big city when I left to go home.

On that first trip, I remember spending the last evening in his one-room flat, playing on the braided rug, pretending it was the island of Manhattan, placing a metal statue of the Empire State Building, which he had bought me as a souvenir, in the center of the concentric ovals and pushing a book, which served as a boat, around the island on the floor. He told me, "There's a boat called the Circle Line, Johnny, that goes around Manhattan. We'll ride it the next time you come to New York—if the weather's good." While I played on the floor, he sang Victor Herbert's "Toyland," a kind of lullaby, a kind of swan song. "Once you pass its borders," he crooned in his wavery tenor voice, "you can never return again." That's how he showed love and regret, sentimental not for his own childhood but for mine.

Back in Mrs. Johnson's class, I showed them my statue of the Empire State Building, but it looked very short. The tip at the top, representing a radio antenna, was bent. I told them about Rockefeller Center, the Believe-It-Or-Not Museum, the ferry, the subway, Times Square, and the Hamburger Train, but I didn't have any pictures to display or candy to distribute, so I think they were disappointed. When I sat down, I felt lonelier than I had ever felt in my life, which I then recognized as divided. I felt different, apart from my classmates, many of them old friends from kindergarten, some of them cousins, who all had homes that did not seem broken like mine. I had basically confessed that my father had left my mother, and my classmates were not interested.

There were so many things I didn't understand. My third-grade class went on a field trip to Easton, about sixteen miles north of Cambridge, to see a movie. I remember one scene in particular: an old man with long white hair, wearing a funny hat with a buckle, something like what the pilgrim fathers wore, climbed up on a horse-drawn wagon in front of a big house with a thatched roof, saying farewell to a young person by the front door. That image of departure haunted me, bothered me. And yet it made me happy to think about it. It wasn't until twenty years later, when I attended a showing of Jean Cocteau's *La Belle et la Bête*, that I saw the same image again. A father was leaving his only child, a daughter, and departing on a long trip that would lead him to the beast and his castle of surrealist special effects, and I realized that the image had stuck with me so glowingly because my own father had left our house recently and wasn't coming back.

My mother started talking openly about what my father had done. "Buck Johnson wanted to call the police. He thought your Daddy had stolen money from the vault. He thought he had embezzled them. I had to talk him into waiting until we heard something from Phil." Buck Johnson, the president of the National Bank of Cambridge, was my godfather—probably an attempt to suck up to the boss. He himself had started as a teller, like my father. Oddly enough, he had served as one of the pallbearers at my grandfather's funeral, which took place in the parlor of the house, not in Christ Church. "Your father owes me a lot," my mother said. "He left in the middle of the night and didn't say a word, didn't leave a note, nothing, but I still stood up for him. Yes, indeed, he owes me, and he owes you too."

Disclosure #4

My father was the odd man out in this trio, matched up against two Carolyns, ultimately a bit player. By leaving, he left them with each other, now a duo, and he left them with me. He became the villain, the provider who had abandoned us, the absent parent I would visit two or three times a year. Their version of events became mine, for he never explained or apologized. As far as I knew, he had run away to New York to become a singer.

Music was the bond that brought these three people together and split them apart. All three were operatic, whether they sang or not. All three were my parents. And I may be talking about their lives, but it's my story.

My Mother's Choice

Not long after my father had moved out of our house in the middle of the night, my mother's 73-year-old uncle started courting her. While his wife was languishing on her deathbed in Philadelphia, Guy Webster was already looking for a replacement. He must have had a fancy for Bayly girls, hoping to keep his amatory and financial interests in the family. During the funeral, he sat with my mother in the family pew, and later he put his arm around her when they stood by Aunt Carrie's open grave in the Bayly corner of the cemetery while Reverend Whatley delivered his benediction. My mother said Uncle Guy was worth fourteen million dollars at the time, but she did tend to exaggerate. Nevertheless, he was clearly rich—and rich in the filthy sense. My mother said his money came from the "syndicate," that he was their front man but was so crooked he had outsmarted them and taken all the loot for himself. She said he owned 2,000 acres of land near Cape Charles, Virginia, just down the Delmarva Peninsula, and ran several tomato canneries. In the grocery store, she showed me labels with the name "Webster" and a picture of a big red tomato.

Clearly my mother had hit a gusher, in terms of financial good fortune, like Pip discovering he had a benefactor in *Great Expectations*, but she was less than half his age. And she was still married to my father, even though they were separated. I didn't understand what kept my parents apart, and my mother didn't discuss it. I didn't make the connection that Carolyn Long might be involved in the break-up.

I liked New York and might have lived there happily, walking to school through the busy, exciting streets, attending baseball games at Yankee Stadium, playing catch with my father in Central Park. Why didn't my mother want to join him there? She told me, "No son of mine is going to live in that dirty city, go to those terrible schools, constantly in danger of his life from those criminals who prowl around those streets, those dope fiends and murderers." Why did my father want to stay in such a place? "He thinks he can be a famous opera singer," my mother scoffed, "but Carolyn told him, 'Phil, you can't sing,' and he didn't want to believe her."

The recent death of Aunt Carrie and a quick divorce from my father would easily remove the obstacles to a union between my young mother and her ancient uncle, who was well endowed financially, at least, and wouldn't, she believed, make any unseemly advances. His mansion was big enough so we'd all have our own bedrooms.

The only mansion I knew about was the plantation house in Walt Disney's *Song of the South*, a film nowadays consigned to the Disney vault because of its racist live-action frame story of a white boy and a kindly old slave, Uncle Remus, who welcomes him in his cabin, tells him stories about Br'er Rabbit, and saves him when a bull attacks as he's crossing a field. I loved the animated parts, the stories of wily Br'er Rabbit and the eternally outwitted bear and fox who try and fail to catch him, the stories that originated in West Africa.

When my mother drove us down to Cheriton, Virginia, to visit Uncle Guy in November, there were no signs of mourning. The house, called Eyreville, was indeed a mansion with brick walls, white pillars, white shutters, and a closed-in porch on the second-floor.

The rooms reminded me of the board game *Clue*. The eighteenth-century house contained a ballroom, a library, a drawing room, and a conservatory. It had an elevator, a grand entry with a talking mynah bird tethered to a cast-iron platform, a dining room with a black marble fireplace and ceilings that were thirteen feet high, an office, a kitchen with two separate sink and stove areas, a pantry with its own fireplace, another kitchen in the back of the house, five bedrooms on the second floor, all with their own fireplaces, dressing rooms, and baths, with two more bedrooms on the third floor (servants' quarters, perhaps). It sat on 1,000 acres of farmland and had over six miles of beach front on the Chesapeake Bay, with six acres of oyster beds. There was a brick octagonal oyster house, with an oven for roasts and the seating capacity for fifty diners, as well as a separate tavern with its own kitchen and bathroom. There were five tenant houses, a cattle shed, three garages, a freezer house, an office building, a pumping station, and a heated, air-conditioned kennel with a run. I made friends with Uncle Guy's dog, a Boxer with cropped ears and docked tail, another inducement for my mother to marry him.

The room in the big house that impressed me the most was the natatorium. The focal point, just off center, was a swimming pool with tiles of aqua and turquoise, a brass railing around the deep end. The pool's runoff gutter around the perimeter was lined with low, leafy plants. There was a skylight directly above the pool. Next to one of the sides, there was a built-in basin of heated sand, so bathers sitting in deck chairs could wiggle their bare feet and pretend they were at the beach. There was a glass tank with a baby alligator. There was a huge brick fireplace with brass andirons. Walls of knotty pine rose to the top of a bank of windows and then canted toward the skylight. There were changing rooms and a walk-in closet stocked with hundreds of bathing suits in all sizes, colors, and patterns. The floor was made of ruddy tiles but covered with a motley collection of rugs. The oddest thing about the room was that it looked essentially like a living room, with plush sofas and easy chairs and wooden rocking chairs in different conversation groups, ship models displayed on mantel and shelves, antique lamps placed on side tables, a chandelier made of electric candles on a huge brass hoop suspended by chains from the ceiling. It was a pleasure dome, a playboy pad, a recreation room, a sybaritic paradise, a child's wonderland. I loved it, but my mother wouldn't let me swim.

"But there are all those suits in there!" I complained.

"Hush, Johnny," she said, "Not now. Not this time. Maybe later. And that's final." Maybe she didn't want to incur too much of a debt or get me too interested in the prospect of living in luxury. Maybe she was simply worried that it was no longer swimming season, even though the pool was indoors and heated. It's possible that I still had a spider bite on the back of my knee and couldn't go in the water. In any case, she was adamant and there was no arguing with her.

Uncle Guy's other way to my heart was to send me outside to ride around the property in a battered yellow golf cart. I even got to drive it myself, up and down the country lane that served as his long driveway. A young man who must have been an employee went with me. As much as I liked driving the chunky vehicle, what I really wanted was to ride on the curved trunk, hanging on to the seat with both hands, and let the car's speed and the wake it created in the air make my body stream back like a flag flying—but really like the cartoon character Huckleberry Hound who held on, each episode, to the back of a speeding roadster as it careened all over the ring of a circus tent. It's remarkable that I didn't fall off—and that the young man allowed me to do something so dangerous—but we must not have been careening as fast as I imagined.

When we drove back home, my mother wasn't sure what to do. Uncle Guy was courting her, wooing her with his wealth, but she couldn't marry him, number one, because she was still married to my father and, number two, because it seemed wrong to marry her uncle, even though he wasn't a blood relation so it wouldn't, strictly speaking, be considered incest. He hadn't proposed, but he did suggest that he wanted to keep his property in the family—and if he ever did formally propose marriage, he would tender her a gift of a million dollars to start with, money that would be hers and hers alone. In terms of the young players then being recruited by major-league baseball teams, it was equivalent to a signing bonus.

Carolyn Long was staying with us in the little house my mother had designed. Even then, when I was eight, I felt that she had replaced my father. I certainly preferred her to creepy old Uncle Guy. She was vivacious, funny, affectionate, and she adored me. But my mother was becoming more and more agitated. She worried about "talk," what everyone was saying. She didn't explain it to me, but I heard enough to understand how uncomfortable she felt with "the whole town watching."

When Carolyn found a teaching position as a professor of vocal arts at the University of Texas, I learned that the three of us were moving to Austin. I was excited, because I loved cowboys and westerns, but I was also afraid, because I had to leave my friends and my hometown in the middle of the school year.

It happened quickly. My mother put our house up for sale and arranged for movers to transfer the furniture and belongings into storage. She and I stayed at my grandmother Sadie's apartment on High Street, while Carolyn spent the last days at Captain Amos's house on Water Street. A girl with a ponytail, whom I thought of as my girlfriend, even in third grade, came by and gave me a present for the long trip: a plastic egg of Silly Putty. My mother rented a U-Haul trailer and had it hooked up to the hitch of our green-and-white Chevrolet Bel-Air. Before we drove off, my mother had me pose for pictures by the trailer. In her snapshots, I look eternally goofy, making faces, striking silly poses, as though we were merely going on vacation. My mother felt we were being driven out of paradise, but it was still a relief to get away from the gossip, still fun to get in the car and drive off in search of new adventures.

We drove past the Academy School, turned at the Yacht Club, and proceeded to High Street, where the car and trailer clattered over bricks. We took a left at the white courthouse, eased around the grimy jail, and crossed the drawbridge over Cambridge Creek. Soon we were driving on the long, low bridge over the Choptank River. Out the side window, since the back was blocked by the trailer, I could see Cambridge growing smaller, the town's name on the water tank becoming unreadable. It was a week before Christmas, and the waves were gray. The bridge held a lot of history. It was named for my grandmother's uncle, Emerson Harrington, who had served as the Governor of Maryland during the First World War. President Franklin Roosevelt had come on his yacht, the Potomac, to christen it. The after-stack now stood at Long Wharf as a memorial. It *looked* like a smokestack, but it was really an elevator, disguised so F.D.R. could move freely and without embarrassment from deck to deck in his wheelchair.

Even in the cold weather of a December morning, Black men were fishing by the concrete railings of the walkways. We drove across the steel truss at the center of the span, and I heard our tires whining over the metal grate. Since the bridge was low, fairly close to the river, there had to be a way for sailboats and other large craft to pass underneath. Instead of a drawbridge, the center section revolved. Carolyn's packet of press releases told the story of how once, late at night, she sang a low note in imitation of a boat's horn, alerting the bridge-keeper to open the bridge. And the bridge swung open so her speedboat, which was little enough to zip under the span at any point, could pass through as if it were a schooner.

Carolyn, who was sitting in the front seat, turned around and said to me, in a very serious, low voice, "Johnny, I want you to remember this. Always. If you ever need me, I promise I'll be there. I'll lie down on the Choptank River bridge and let a Mack truck run over me before I'll let you down. Don't you ever forget that."

She never let me forget that. All she had to do was mention a Mack truck or the bridge over the Choptank River, and I knew what she meant. "Your own father left," she said, "and now I have to be your father."

After we crossed the long bridge into Talbot County, my mother laughed and called out, "Ah, river!" It was their way of saying *au revoir*. Carolyn repeated it, "Ah, river, and good riddance." We headed up Route 50, which was then a two-lane highway running between thick stands of loblolly pines, like a lane through the Black Forest in the Grimms' fairy tales I loved, in particular the one about the Bremen Town Musicians, a group of worn-out animals who scared a gang of thieves from their hideout in the forest by standing one atop the other outside their window. We were like those animals running away from a home where we were no longer wanted, looking for a safe haven. "We're the Three Musty Rears," Carolyn announced. "All for one and one for all."

We drove past landmarks I knew from earlier trips, stopping at Whispering Pines, a roadhouse in a clearing of tall trees where Buck Bryan sold whiskey. Carolyn went in, while my mother and I waited in the idling car, and came out with a loaded bag. We drove past the drive-in movie theatre at Trappe, the barn with a blue roof, the octagonal meeting house, and the ruins of a brick church from Colonial days. When the towers of the Chesapeake Bay Bridge came into view, I remembered how scared I used to be, worried that we were going to drive right up the cables of the suspension bridge. When we swooped up to the top, we'd keep going until we plunged into the bay and drowned.

We stopped at a restaurant with a Dutch windmill turning on its roof and ate lunch. I could never resist a juke box, so I played "Standing on the Corner, Watching All the Girls Go By," thinking of my ponytailed girlfriend and already, at eight years old, feeling sappy about romantic love. At the counter on our way out, my mother bought me a pair of magnetic dogs, black and white Scotties, that made me start begging her for a real dog.

In those days, before the Capital Beltway was built, we had to drive through Washington, D.C., but that was a treat for me because our route on Pennsylvania Avenue took us past the Capitol and the White House. I couldn't have guessed how much of our real future we were driving through, crossing over the District line at Friendship Heights and entering Bethesda, where we passed St. John's Episcopal Church (where I would eventually sing in the choir as a boy soprano) and turning onto Old Georgetown Road at the Bank of Bethesda (where my mother would eventually work as head teller), a stone wedge of a building that faced the intersection like a ship's prow in dry dock. We ended up at the brick house of Grandfather and Grandmother Drury on Spruce Tree Avenue, where we spent the first night of our journey. My father may have left us, but we showed up at his parents' house, depending on them for our first port of call, our real point of debarkation from the familiar into the unknown.

We had a booklet of road maps from AAA, with a thick yellow line marking the best route to Austin. The next day, we planned to head south through Virginia, cutting across Tennessee, Alabama, Mississippi, Louisiana, and finally into Texas. My mother did all of the driving, since Carolyn didn't have a valid license, and she said, "My limit's 200 miles a day." We would stay at a lot of motels on the 1,600 mile trip to Texas.

We posed for more pictures on the driveway by Granddaddy's garage. I was climbing up the trailer, horsing around, and grinning like Lon Chaney in a silent horror movie. And then I was sitting on a red bicycle, one of my few belongings from home. In the back seat, I rode with the stuffed terrier I was given when I had my tonsils out. The doctor assured me that he had removed the toy dog's tonsils too.

Our progress was leisurely. We made a detour soon after we began, driving into the Shenandoah Valley and visiting the Virginia Military Institute in Lexington.

"Blair the Pear went to school here," Carolyn said.

"That was Carrie's first husband," my mother added.

"Yes, indeed, he was a Lieutenant Colonel in the Marines. He landed on Iwo Jima and led his battalion ashore through a typhoon of machine-gun fire. When I got his letters, I had to shake out volcanic ash. He brought back a Japanese flag. I'll give it to you when we get settled and don't have to live out of a suitcase."

She took a long draw on the cigarette she was holding.

"When I was through with him, I married Duke the Puke. He was a cowboy."

"Did he live in Texas?" I asked.

"No, my darling, he punched cattle on the King Ranch in Cuba. But he was originally from Colorado and attended one of my concerts there in the Rocky Mountains. After that, he followed me from concert to concert. When we got to Elkton, Maryland, he married me."

"They were both rich," my mother said.

"Yes, but Blair was an aristocrat. Came from old Virginia gentility." It didn't occur to me until I was an adult that the nickname for her first husband might have been "Blair the Pair," as in the command, "Sound off like you got a pair!"

We visited the museum of the military academy, where we saw a stuffed horse from the Civil War. It stood in the middle of a gallery, wearing a bridle, as though waiting to be saddled indoors. "That's Traveller," my mother told me, "He was the horse of Robert E. Lee."

"Looks like they forgot to use mothballs," Carolyn said. Neither one liked to waste time reading labels or they would have realized that the mounted hide was in fact Little Sorrel, the horse of Stonewall Jackson, kept on display because the General had taught there as a Professor of Natural and Experimental Philosophy, as well as an Instructor of Artillery, before the War between the States. Maybe they were confused because General Lee had ended his days in Lexington as President of Washington College, later renamed Washington and Lee. Maybe, at one of the gift shops we browsed through on our way to Texas, my mother had bought a postcard of the General sitting on Traveller. For years, she would claim that we'd seen Robert E. Lee's moth-eaten horse.

When we drove through Bristol, a city that's half in Virginia and half in Tennessee, I saw a store with a sign for "BAGELS."

"What's that?" I said. "What are bagels?"

Carolyn turned halfway around in her seat, so she could look at me, and made a joke: "They're Jewish doughnuts, my darling."

"Carolyn!" my mother snapped, while Carolyn laughed. "Don't go teasing the boy like that. Tell him what they really are."

"They're delicious," Carolyn said, "Heavenly. Scrumptious. But not sweet. You eat them with lox—that's smoked salmon—and a dollop of cream cheese. Best thing you ever tasted. The best place to get them, old bean, is in New York City, in a delicatessen."

I was so ignorant, even at eight years old, I didn't know what "Jewish" meant. "They're the Israelites in the Bible," my mother explained. "Jesus Christ was Jewish."

"Then why aren't we?" Although she had taught Sunday school at Christ Church and liked to tell people that she had been baptized in water from the River Jordan, she had no answer for that.

Carolyn and I pleaded with her to go back to the bakery so we could pick up a bag of bagels, along with some cream cheese and lox, and have brunch at one of the picnic tables we passed on the two-lane highways we traveled, but with a U-Haul trailer behind our Chevy, my mother refused to make a

U-turn. She kept on driving, heading for her 200-mile limit.

When we saw a big sign for "Stuckey's PECAN Shoppe," we pulled off the highway and stopped. Even though the car wasn't especially low on gas—I looked over my mother's shoulder at the gauge and it was half full—my mother cranked down her window and told the attendant to "fill her up with High-Test." While he cleaned the windshield, spraying it with blue fluid and wiping it with a rag, and then propped up the hood to check the oil level and the radiator, we browsed for novelties and souvenirs inside the store.

I found a cardboard plaque with samples of minerals—chunks of pink quartz, granite, shale, mica—and handed it to my mother so she could buy it for me. Since I was always leaning forward in the back seat, asking her where we were going, reminding her when the needle of the speedometer wavered above 55 miles-per-hour, telling her "You're driving too fast, Mom, you're over the speed limit," she bought me a Back Seat Driver's License, which I filled out when we got back in the car, printing my name on the blank line.

But Carolyn was even more vocal about the unsafe driving habits of other motorists on the two-lane highways we traveled. Whenever she thought someone had cut us off or stopped too abruptly at a traffic signal or failed to yield right of way, she rolled down her window, stuck out her head so the wind made her curly black hair blow around, and shouted, *"Lazzarone brutto!"* I didn't know that it meant "Ugly scoundrel!" but I knew it was an insult.

"Now, the truckers are friendly, my darling," she told me. "When you pass them, they flash their headlights so you know it's safe to pull back over from the passing lane. They look out for other drivers. They signal when state troopers are looking for speeders, so you don't get a ticket. They also know the best places to eat."

In Tennessee, we made a detour to visit the cabin—or a replica of the cabin—where Davy Crockett was born, not exactly on a "mountain top," as the theme song of the Disney show declared, but more on a little hill. Like many boys of the time, I had caught the frontier bug and had worn a fringed buckskin jacket and a coonskin cap, with a powder horn slung over one shoulder and a musket named Betsy slung over the other.

Whenever I became impatient that we weren't making faster progress to Texas, Carolyn replied, *"La Roma non fu fatta in un giorno,"* more of the Italian she had learned when she was studying opera and singing in Milan. When I persisted, she turned around slowly to give me a threatening look, pulling down her sunglasses and opening her bug eyes wider, and said in a low voice, *"Basta!"*

I enjoyed staying in motels, which often advertised themselves as motor courts, usually a string of rooms, like a train behind the locomotive of the main office where we checked in. Sometimes the rooms were separate cottages, each with its own pitched roof, but usually they were connected. One motel had an office in what looked like a red brick plantation house, with white pillars on a two-story portico and wings of rooms branching out from either side. I loved exploring the grounds, looking for horseshoes around the metal prongs and dirt patches of the pits, trying to play by myself on a see-saw, pretending I was a pioneer in the groves of pine trees, dropping coins in the wishing wells, wishing it were still summer and I could swim in the pool (if the motel had one) or lounge in the hammock that hung twisted between tree trunks.

I was whining about how I wanted a dog, so my mother, who saw a hand-printed sign at a gas station near Knoxville, drove off the highway up a dirt road to a ramshackle cabin on a hilltop in the woods. We adopted a pedigreed beagle puppy, and I named him, after my two previous dogs, Herbert. From then on, we had to sneak the dog into our motel rooms and try to keep him from baying or whimpering or peeing on the carpet. It amused Carolyn and annoyed my mother that I kept on crooning, "You ain't nothin' but a hound dog."

By late afternoon, when it was already getting dark, we were all on the lookout for the flashing neon signs of motels. When we got close enough, we checked to see if the word NO was lit up in front of VACANCY. If it was, we all groaned. "I'm tired," my mother said, "I'm just about worn out."

We always got two rooms, one for me and one that my mother and Carolyn shared, sometimes with a connecting door between them. On Christmas Eve, we checked into a motel around Chattanooga. We had to sneak the beagle in and try to keep him quiet. Carolyn and my mother made him sleep on a pillow they placed in the corner, next to layers of newspaper. They put an alarm clock next to his curled-up body and covered him with a towel. My mother went out by herself and came back with an artificial Christmas tree, which she set up on the desk in my room. "Santa will bring you presents," she assured me, even though I didn't see a fireplace by which he could enter the motel. "He can park his sleigh in the parking lot," she said. "We'll leave the door unlocked so he can let himself in." In the morning, when I woke up in the strange room, lights were glittering on the little tree, and there were several presents, all unwrapped, on the desktop. The biggest one was an elaborate crystal radio made of black plastic, with all sorts of dials and lights and buttons and sliders. I never did figure out how to use it.

We got all the way to Tuscaloosa, Alabama, before my mother couldn't go any farther. "I don't want to keep on driving," she said between sobs, "I just don't. Please, Carolyn, please let's go back." They told me to go play outside our motel room. As it grew darker and cooler, I walked up and down the bench of a picnic table in a pine grove, leaping off and then walking up and down the bench on the opposite side, pushing away pine needles with my shoes, playing some sort of game I had invented. The headlights of cars and trucks passed on the highway, and the sound of their engines grew fainter until it was quiet again. Carolyn came out and said, "There you are, old bean. Get yourself inside. Your mother says it's pneumonia weather."

We couldn't go all the way back to Cambridge, Maryland, but we retraced our route to Birmingham and checked into the Essex House, where my mother and Carolyn circled want ads in the newspaper. We never did get to Texas. I'm not sure what happened to Carolyn's teaching position at the university in Austin. Perhaps it was wishful thinking all along, a figment based on a musical acquaintance who might have offered assistance to a lady in distress. She had been a real diva, giving hundreds of concerts all over the United States and Canada, but now she was unemployed, like my mother, two women with a small boy in a city that was strange to all of us. We had entered the unknown, and it was no longer exactly an adventure.

I stood at the window of the hotel and gazed at the lights of Birmingham, Alabama. On Red Mountain, a statue of the Roman god Vulcan guarded the city. Carolyn explained that he was the protector of blacksmiths and stood there because of the steel mills. I remember the statue as glowing, a fiery red, but actually it was gray, made of iron mined locally. I might have misremembered the color because he held a beacon that flashed red or green, depending on traffic conditions below the promontory.

We moved into the second floor of a wooden house on 34th Street South, where I slept on a sofa in the living room. A kitchen separated my sleeping quarters from the bedroom Carolyn and my mother shared at the rear of the house. My favorite thing about the apartment was the fire escape, which reminded me of the stairs behind a western saloon.

After New Year's Day in 1959, I resumed third grade in a new school, Lakeview Elementary. It confused me because we changed classrooms every hour, and I couldn't remember where to go. I couldn't remember the way to school in the morning, getting lost and trudging home for a ride. It wasn't long before I pretended I was lost so I could return to my mother, making sure I was tardy. I hadn't missed that much school, since most of our trip had taken place during Christmas vacation, but I was seriously behind.

Carolyn was looking for a job, and we spent one afternoon at a musician's house, sitting in a room with French windows and a grand piano. She and Bobby sipped cocktails while I drank a glass of lemonade. Carolyn exuded her vivacious, flirtatious best, dropping names like Lanza, Pinza, and Ormandy, touting her mastery of her Maestro's method of teaching singers how to produce a pure tone, but the musician, a choir director, advised her to build up her own private studio. He would try to find her some solo work in the local churches, but he didn't know how much they paid.

Neither she nor my mother could find any kind of employment. I'm not sure how hard they tried. We were stuck in the little apartment in a run-down house, trying to act like a family, with a beagle puppy whining, barking, and howling, half paper-trained. He was my dog, but I never walked him. My mother had to do it, and she wasn't especially fond of dogs.

They tried to find me friends, and I went with some kids to a couple of movies, one about the pirate Jean Lafitte at the Battle of New Orleans and one about the only survivor of the Seventh Cavalry at the Battle of Little Big Horn, a horse named Comanche. Our home sounded more and more like a battlefield, with nightly explosions from the other room, voices rising to shrieks and subsiding to weeping. Sometimes I heard glass breaking or the back door slamming, but they never burst into the living room. They tried to atone for the conflict by pampering me, letting me stay up late to watch my favorite television show, *The Rifleman*, starring Chuck Connors, who played the widowed father of an only child, a sad-faced boy with whom I identified. I don't think I consciously missed my own father, but I wanted someone like a cowboy or a baseball player (which Chuck Connors had been) who could show me what to do.

We didn't last longer than a month in Birmingham. My mother got in touch with Uncle Guy, who was uglier than Vulcan but rich from his tomato canneries, and said she was reconsidering the proposal he had suggested during our visit to his mansion on the Eastern Shore of Virginia. She had tried one extreme. Now she was ready to swing toward the other. Carolyn was devastated, staying in bed like someone sick with a cold, but at least things were quieter at night, since they weren't speaking to each other. They were breaking up.

It was a sad day when my mother and I took Carolyn to the terminal in Birmingham and put her on a train back to Washington. She had a compartment to herself, and it looked, as she said "adorable, in the high style I was used to when I was touring." Both she and my mother were wiping away tears. "Bobby," Carolyn said, "you're ruining my makeup. Now I'll have to put on my face again." She started powdering her cheeks and penciling in her eyebrows and was reapplying mascara as we left the compartment and walked down the corridor. When we gazed at her window as the train started moving, she was looking at us sadly, like a little girl who had done something wrong but didn't know what, waving her hand feebly, as though trying to clutch something she couldn't hold.

We gave away our beagle to a breeder. Later, when we returned north,

I wrote a letter, stating in the most formal language I could summon that he had promised to give us the pick of the litter when our beagle, Herbert, sired some offspring, and now, if they didn't ship us a puppy post haste, we would be forced to sue. I never got a reply—I'm not sure my mother ever posted the letter—just as I never received the combination compass and decoder I had ordered by cutting out box tops from cereal boxes and mailing them to Minneapolis, Minnesota. We had left no forwarding address at our second-floor apartment in Birmingham. We didn't know where we would end up.

Uncle Guy resumed his pursuit of his niece. He met us in Birmingham and took us on vacation to Florida. He drove my mother's car while I rode in his Mercury, driven by his Black chauffeur, who talked with me about baseball. I wondered why, if he was so rich, Uncle Guy didn't own a Cadillac.

Right away, as a token of his good intentions, he gave my mother a mink stole with her first name, Carolyn, stitched in script letters on the silk lining. I noticed that he never called her Bobby. He was careful to address her as Carolyn, the same name as that of his recently deceased wife, for whom my mother was named. For all I know, it might have been Aunt Carrie's stole he was passing along.

When we stopped along the way, I was happy to see my mother again and gave her a big hug, but I also started to pay attention to Uncle Guy, my prospective stepfather. He seemed friendly enough, even though his expression was squinty and a little frightening. He had what my mother called a "hard face," with a hawkish nose, a strong jaw, and a head that looked more threatening because he was pretty much bald on top, with some stringy hairs plastered down toward a thicker fringe. I thought of my father's full head of hair, which he was very proud of and spent a lot of time combing, especially in public, whenever we went in a restaurant or onto a subway. Uncle Guy was taller and huskier than my father.

He made sure I was entertained along the way. It was late January, and even sunny Florida seemed a little cool. We stopped at Silver Springs and looked at flamingos but didn't ride the glass-bottom boats. We stopped at a Seminole village with thatched huts. They didn't look like the Plains Indians I knew from westerns on television: no feathered headdresses, no ponies, no tomahawks, no bows and arrows, no warpaint. The Seminoles wore striped shirts, scarves, and no hats at all.

I was disappointed to learn that we were staying in Miami, not Miami Beach. We could see water from our hotel room, but it wasn't the ocean. I can't remember what we did for fun, but we did go out one evening to a movie palace and saw *A Hole in the Head*, a romantic comedy in which Frank Sinatra and a little boy ("Look at him! Precious! He's your age, Johnny!") sang the song "High Hopes," the one about "Oops! There goes another rubber-tree plant."

Uncle Guy had high hopes, but so did my mother and I. We liked the idea of having a lot of money. It was a real temptation. I probably spent most of our time in Miami in the hotel room my mother and I shared, reading through a stack of comic books and watching television. My mother and Uncle Guy were deep in negotiations in his room. In the segregated south, the chauffeur had to stay in the Black section of town.

On our last night, my mother returned to our room and sat me down on one of the twin beds to explain what she had decided. What passed between us happened a long time ago, but she repeated it over and over through the years that followed. From the start, she paid no attention to how old I was, treating me like an adult even when I was a bewildered third-grader, even when I couldn't possibly understand the full import of her revelations and justifications. She was trying to convince herself she had done the right thing, citing what her mother, Sadie, whom she called by her first name, and her sister Sarah has advised her to do.

"Sadie made me swear on a stack of Bibles I wouldn't marry Guy Webster. It was simply wrong. He was my uncle. He was too old. But then she thought about it, talked it over with her gossipy friends, and decided that maybe it was okay after all. I was welcome to do whatever I thought was right. I could get a quickie divorce in Nevada or Mexico or somewhere sunny and could start living in the fashion I deserved, what my training as a young lady had prepared me to do with my life. The marriage had her blessing."

She stopped to tap out a Kent, lit it with a silver lighter, and took a deep puff. "Aunt Sarah said, 'Bobby, you're a fool if you don't marry Guy. Then you could give me a thousand dollars every Christmas.'" I already knew that Aunt Sarah had married not just one but *two* men for their money.

"I was ready to say yes," she continued, "but then he said, 'I expect you to be a wife in every sense of the word.' I was ready to accept his proposal until he said that. I thought he was too old to be interested in *that*. I couldn't imagine sleeping with that old man. It gave me the creeps. I can still feel my skin crawling. I thought he wanted companionship, someone with a little education, a good conversationalist, a hostess who knew about etiquette, who knew where the silverware went at a proper table setting. I thought he wanted a real lady. Boy, was I mistaken."

She said that Uncle Guy wanted to send me off to boarding school in England so I could become a proper gentleman. Of course, if he did that I'd be out of the house, the mansion we had visited in November, so I wouldn't have much chance to swim in the natatorium or tool around in the golf cart or play with the dog or talk with the mynah bird.

"He wanted you to take his family name, Webster. And if we changed your last name, I was going to insist on changing your first name too, so you'd be Alexander, after my father. Sadie was upset I didn't do that when you were born. I'd call you Alec."

She was willing to take his millions, but she refused to sleep with him and be his wife in every sense of the word. Someone else would do it, though, she assured me. "It would have killed me. I would have drunk myself to death."

Carolyn Long must have had something to do with my mother's revulsion and her rejection of the old man's proposal. Both of them probably saw this courtship as a betrayal, but I can now see, in my mother's machinations, the plot for a novel by Henry James, in which my mother would accept the millions but meet her "cousin" for secret rendezvous. Eventually Carolyn would move into the mansion at Eyreville. Maybe Uncle Guy's money could finance her comeback as an opera singer. How long could he live, anyway? He was in his seventies. Surely she could wear him down—although preferably not in bed.

The last thing I remember about Miami is a travel agency where my mother bought our tickets. I looked at a model airplane, lettered in red for TWA, in the store-front window, but the agent said he was sorry he wasn't allowed to give it to the nice boy. Outside, where I waited, I noticed how sandy the streets were, how bare the landscape. The streets seemed to go nowhere, past little white houses with scrubby plants in the yards.

My first airplane ride was on a National Airlines DC-7, a propeller plane flying from Miami to Washington, D.C. (Carolyn's destination when we put her on the train). I was fascinated by the inflatable life jackets stowed under the seats. I liked them so much, my mother stole one for me, stuffing it into her big pocketbook. When we unpacked our suitcases and she showed it off, proud of her talent for larceny, I was so embarrassed that I made her promise to return it to the airline, but I'm sure she threw it away.

She never felt entirely comfortable about keeping the mink stole, but she did wear it whenever she went to some restaurant that was swanky and wanted to impress people. Eventually, though, a sense of guilt led her to give it away to one of the housekeepers she continued to employ long after she had become poor herself.

When we arrived in Washington, my mother and I took a taxi from the airport to my grandparents' house on Spruce Tree Avenue, where we had spent a night before our ill-fated journey to Alabama and Florida. The surprise was that Carolyn Long was already staying there.

Disclosure #5

I'm able to add up the rooms of Uncle Guy's mansion and the outbuildings and the acres of arable land and the miles of bay front and the number of window panes on the second-floor façade thanks to a brochure from Sotheby Parke Bernet, which offered the property for sale at $1,500,000 in 1977. In today's dollars, based on inflation, it would be worth about $7,700,000.

My mother stapled a photograph to her copy of the auction house's brochure. She stands on one of the wide brick steps before the mansion's screen porch, Aunt Carrie on one side and Uncle Guy on the other. All three are smiling widely, but only my mother and Aunt Carrie are looking at the photographer. Uncle Guy is leering at my mother, who wasn't my mother then but a young brunette fresh from high school. His interest seems more than avuncular—a little lascivious, a little proprietary.

Broken Music

On a cold afternoon in early spring, Carolyn bundled herself up like a sailor in a squall and walked along the street where we lived in Bethesda, Maryland, past apartment buildings named Glenwood, Glenmont, and Glenbrook, past the courtyards and parking lots of garden apartments, and then past a stretch of the street that still contained houses, trying to round up friends for me. I heard the story for the rest of her life: "You didn't have any playmates, so I marched up and down Battery Lane, huddled in my peacoat, and whenever I saw some boys playing, I called out, 'Which of you needs a playmate?'"

Carolyn lived with my mother and me in a one-bedroom apartment in a recently constructed building named Glen Aldon. It was brick, several stories tall, with a dark inner corridor as well as outside doors for the first-floor apartments. The name was applied in white script to the wall next to a grand entrance with a semi-circular driveway and a concrete canopy that slanted jazzily upward, supported by black metal struts with a series of rings that got bigger as they rose, held in by straight metal beams, like bubbles going up a straw. In the absence of trees to climb, I liked to ascend those circles like a ladder and touch the high canopy.

The construction was so new that the lawn outside our door was bare earth when we moved in. I watched as workers tossed rolls of sod off a truck and unspooled them like grassy masking tape over the dirt, kneeling and pushing them forward. You could see the seams between strips of sod.

My grandmother had evicted Carolyn because of her flirting with Granddaddy, an economist who suffered from Parkinson's Disease. Carolyn called him "Maestro," touching his shaking arm, performing snatches of arias at the piano, cooing about how much she admired intellectuals, men with "brains you could pick." When my mother found a job working as a teller at a branch of the Bank of Bethesda, not too far down Old Georgetown Road, we were able to move out and reunite with Carolyn, who had been staying at the YWCA downtown. The two women signed a one-year lease for the apartment we shared. My mother told me, many years later, that they had to call themselves "cousins" in order to rent a place together as two women without husbands.

Susie Vernon was the resident manager, and she lived on our floor down the inner hallway with her redheaded sister and her daughter, Little Susie, who was my baby sitter and eventually taught me how to dance, demonstrating the box step in one of the building's storerooms. "She isn't really her sister," my mother explained. "Can't you tell? They don't look a thing like each other." Even then, it occurred to me that Carolyn might not really be our cousin.

I remember two things about Susie Vernon. My mother gave her a painting I loved. At our house in Cambridge, it had hung over the upright piano. It depicted a thunderstorm at sea, a sailing ship foundering on some rocks, and a lifeboat of conquistadors battling the towering waves to reach the safety of land. I thought that they would succeed in rowing ashore, pulling up on a beach littered with debris. And then, in my mind, the story merged into one of my favorite picture books, *The Sailor Dog*, and I imagined the conquistadors, still in their shiny helmets and breast-plates, gathering driftwood and nailing crooked pieces together to build little houses on the sand.

The other thing I remember is my mother telling me how Carolyn got Susie to take her to Woodward and Lothrop's, a department store that everyone called Woodie's, and spent a lot of money on a collection of wax fruit: red and green apples, an orange, a lemon, green and yellow pears, strawberries, grapes, walnuts, and two bananas. They were shockingly realistic, the apples having a shine while the bananas did not, the textures accurate, with nubbly seeds on the skin of the strawberries and pocked indentations on the rind of the citrus fruits. Even the stems were convincing. Every piece looked different. The shapes seemed to be sculpted by hand. "I was so mad," my mother told me, "I could have spit. I said, 'Carolyn, are you out of your mind? Spending over two hundred dollars on a bunch of wax fruit?' But they were beautiful. They looked good enough to eat."

Artificial seems too demeaning a word for those beauties that still occupy a silver *repoussé* bowl with a fancy handle on top of a drop-leaf table. They also had an important place in the intimate relationship between my mother and Carolyn, but I didn't find out exactly what that entailed until the last year of my mother's life.

The friends Carolyn found for me didn't stick. The friends I found for myself—Jimmy, Chuck, and Carla, the blonde tomboy—lived with single mothers in the same chain of apartment buildings. We had one thing in common: we all came from broken homes, although mine had been reassembled with a new set of parents: two women with a boy in the 1950s.

We formed a sandlot baseball team, calling ourselves the Battery Lane Bombers, and played on the grounds of N.I.H., the National Institutes of Health, where a golf course used to be located. We had to shimmy under a chain-link fence where it passed over a dry streambed to reach the backstop and diamond, and we had to look out for the "paddy wagon" that came to chase kids away. My mother made friends with their mothers—Alberta, Lily, and Hazel—and kept them more faithfully than I kept mine.

We wondered about the name Battery Lane. Did it refer to an electrical battery? Assault and battery? But we finally realized that it must have stemmed from the Civil War, when fortifications surrounded Washington and an artillery battery positioned its cannons along the ridgeline that the curving street followed.

Life, in any case, was full of electricity and violence on Battery Lane. I moved away when I went to college, returning sporadically when, like the old farmhand in Robert Frost's "The Death of the Hired Man," I had nowhere else to go and Battery Lane represented "the place where, when you have to go there,/They have to take you in." My mother would continue to live there, in one apartment or another, for almost three decades, minus a three-year period when all three of us rented a house on Massachusetts Avenue. "Of all the places I've lived," she said near the end of her life, "I'd have to say I was happiest on Battery Lane." I'm sure she felt the most freedom there—although if she had been rich, she would have felt even freer in Barbados. Bethesda offered her the least distance between what she *should* do and what she really *wanted* to do. The warring impulses pulled her apart for her entire life. She left the freedom of Battery Lane twenty years before she died, another paradise lost—but a paradise not of innocence but of experience, as stormy as the painting of the shipwreck and the conquistadors rowing to safety, a paradise of intensity, not calm.

I slept on a daybed in the dining room, using an antique corner cupboard in place of a dresser. I learned to love going to bed early, once Carolyn gave me a new stuffed dog, a basset hound I could cuddle through the night, along with the terrier whose tonsils were supposedly removed when I had mine taken out in the hospital. When she thought I was too excited and would have trouble sleeping, Carolyn took a pair of scissors and snipped a yellow capsule in half. Even though the scissors had pinched it shut, I could still taste the bitter powder before I took a sip of water and swallowed my half of the medicine.

Movers had brought my mother's furniture out of storage. My mother and Carolyn shared one of the tester beds (which my mother pronounced "TEE-ster"). It had four dark wooden posts, probably oak, with a frilly white canopy on top and white curtains below the side rails and foot rails, like little skirts.

The living room doubled as Carolyn's voice studio. She had a reel-to-reel tape recorder next to the upright piano. There was an old-fashioned phonograph by the door that opened to the side yard, a pier glass mirror by the door that led to the inner hallway. The furniture was antique: marble, mahogany, blue glass globes on the lamps, green velvet on the curvy Victorian sofa. Over the window was a gold cornice with crests. It was a gift from Betsy Patterson to my great-great-great grandfather, Josiah Bayly, who served as her attorney when she divorced Napoleon's brother Jerome. The crests were the Bonaparte seal.

Carolyn set out to educate me. "You've never heard of Hitler? *Mamma mia*," she exclaimed, "he was the most evil man ever spawned on this planet."

"Your daddy fought in the army against the Nazis," my mother said. "They gave him a medal because he happened to be twenty miles from a battle."

"Yes, indeed, another son of a bitch," Carolyn said. "You certainly know how to pick them, my dear. Sometimes, as they say, love lights on a cow turd."

That was one of their maxims, and I heard it frequently through the years as a way to explain the inexplicable, the mystery of how someone's love could land on an unworthy object of affection, like Titania falling for Nick Bottom when he's been transformed into an ass.

Carolyn decided that my vocabulary needed improvement, so she began to introduce new words like *procrastinate* (since I always put off doing what I was supposed to do, like carrying the trash cans down the hall and dumping them into the incinerator chute, hating how cigarette ashes wafted into the air) and *cogitate* (since I didn't think before I did something noisy and disruptive, like throwing my baseball against the brick of the apartment building, playing catch with myself).

"Darling, my sweet cookie-wookie," Carolyn said, "it's vitally important for you to form good habits, now while you're young, so I want you to make a habit of looking up words you don't know in the dictionary and make up sentences using them. For example, you should know the word *pusillanimous*, meaning spineless. 'Your father is a pusillanimous worm.'"

Her love of words included word play, so the glass of milk she slowly poured and offered me was always *milky dilkers*. One of the bottles of bourbon they kept on a table in the living room was labeled Cabin Still, but in the evening Carolyn always asked for a snort of "Stab 'n' Kill." She was trying to educate Bobby as well, and when my mother died I found scraps of paper with lists of new words that Carolyn had assigned: *panache, hyperbole, pulchritudinous, superfluous, tenuous, ambiguity, pedantic, convoluted, convivial, semantics, proclivities, accoutrements.*

After her cat Luigi squatted in the litter box, which was a black roasting pan, and pawed around the sand to cover up what he'd deposited, he sat on the oriental rug and lifted up one hind leg while he licked his rear end. "See that?" Carolyn said. "He's playing the bass fiddle." She looked at her fat tiger cat with adoration and said: "Isn't he fastidious about his poop chute? When I was living in Milano, I poured spaghetti on newspapers and he devoured it. I saved him from being eaten. It was so cold, and the neighbors were so poor. '*Per favore, signorina,*' they begged, but I told them 'No! *Basta!* You'll have to eat me first!'"

She was educating my mother about music too. Since she was an opera singer herself and had performed the lead role in the first opera in the English language ever produced in Barcelona—Henry Purcell's *Dido and Aeneas*—she had the authority to make pronouncements. Once, at a recital of Joan Sutherland's ("back when she was thin," my mother liked to say, "so you *know* that was a long time ago"), Carolyn could not tolerate what she was hearing, so she let out a low, loud "Mah!" and walked out in the middle of an aria, my mother following her, muttering "Excuse me" as she moved down the row and then scurrying after Carolyn up the aisle to the lobby. "I've never been more embarrassed in my life!" she said, but she loved to recount the story of how domineering a critic Carolyn could be.

My mother had always adored Jeanette MacDonald, the soprano with a sweet, light, trilling voice who starred in operettas and movies, often paired with the baritone Nelson Eddy. I still have the scrapbook my mother kept, with photographs of the singer and clippings pasted to the crumbling pages. It surprises me that the scrapbook survived that first apartment on Battery Lane, but it was probably packed in a steamer trunk in the building's storeroom.

Every evening, cocktails began to flow at five o'clock sharp, "when the sun dropped under the yardarm." Bobby and Carolyn might end any given evening in lovey-dovey cooing, but they might also end it in mutual, sullen silence or in volleys of screaming. I liked to go to bed early, cuddling my stuffed basset hound and stuffed terrier, in the hope that the two women would retire to the bedroom, where the closed door would muffle any commotion.

One night, I fell asleep happily on my daybed in the dining room, but I woke up to the sound of something breaking in the adjacent living room. It sounded like a china plate falling off a table onto the parquet floor. I turned my head and heard another crash. A light was glowing in the living room. I got out of bed and walked around the drop-leaf table. I heard another crash.

"Mom?" I said. She was sitting on the oriental rug in a pool of black lily pads, her collection of 78 r.p.m. phonograph records. She lifted one up, looked at the label, and then smashed it on the wooden floor next to the rug. She was sobbing. "Mom?"

"Carrie made me do it," she whimpered. "She said she couldn't sing. Jeanette MacDonald couldn't sing. I couldn't take it anymore, so I'm getting rid of her records."

She continued to smash the fragile black disks on the floor. Shards like slick black knives were piling up in front of her. Carolyn emerged from the bedroom.

"Bobby, she can't sing, and that's all there is to it. I ought to know. You *cain't* put it where it *ain't*." Carolyn stood in the middle of the room, wearing a black kimono with white flowers sewn into the silk, not approaching any closer. "The sparrows in a bush outside sound better than she does with that quaver in her voice. You call that a voice? The lowest man on the totem pole sings better than she does."

My mother kept on wailing and smashing her records.

"Mom, please. Don't do it. Don't break them. Please don't break your records. You love them."

"I know I do, but Carrie doesn't approve, so I'm going to do it anyway, one by one, until they're gone."

"Don't make a spectacle of yourself," Carolyn said, her voice low, her movements deliberate, as if in slow-motion, "not in front of your son."

My mother's wailing got louder, her face bright red, her short hair in curlers, fuzzy slippers on her little feet. Carolyn turned around and retreated to the bedroom, shutting the door behind her. I stood, shifting my weight from one foot to the other, and watched until my mother ran out of records. When she was finished, she gave me a fierce, long hug and tucked me back into bed. "I'll get us out of here," she said, "I promise." She was still crying, but not so explosively. As I tried to get back to sleep, hugging my two stuffed dogs, I heard her sweeping the pieces into a grocery bag.

She may have been drinking, but she didn't leave a pile of broken records on the floor that night. After breakfast the next morning, before I walked to school, she had me carry the heavy bag down the hall to the trash room. When I opened up the drawer in the wall and shoved in the bag, I heard the broken pieces smashing once again as they trundled down the chute and crashed at the bottom of the incinerator.

Disclosure #6

"I was always the one who left," my mother said when she was confined to a nursing home, explaining how she had instigated every break-up with Carolyn. "We just didn't get along. She said I really wasn't her type. I wasn't good enough for her."

For a period of nearly thirty years, they lived in eight different apartments on Battery Lane, only the first and the last together. They may have resided on opposite sides of the street or across a parking lot, but they paid regular conjugal visits. Even though they clashed and pulled away from each other, they couldn't break the magnetic attraction. The physics of their difficult relationship demanded proximity.

Separate Residences

In 1960, when I was finishing fourth grade, my mother and I moved across Battery Lane to a ground-floor apartment in the Glenwood building, while Carolyn moved to the other end of Glen Aldon. Both apartments had two bedrooms and strips of grass running by the outside doors. Both had silver boxes by the doors to the inner corridors where a milkman delivered Embassy milk.

It made the daily routine of work and school much calmer, much easier. Bobby and Carolyn got along better when they lived in separate apartments, although my mother and I still spent a lot of time at Carolyn's place. They liked to set up an aluminum charcoal grill on the narrow strip of grass next to the parking lot, marinate chunks of sirloin, and stick them on skewers, along with cherry tomatoes, baby onions, slices of green pepper, mushrooms, and wedges of cut oranges. My mother and I often slept over at Carolyn's apartment.

When I wanted to open a lemonade stand, Carolyn suggested that I call it "Johnny's Greasy Spoon." I thought it was a horrible name, since I didn't know that diners were called "greasy spoons" and didn't get the joke. I set up the stand, really a card table with a sign, a cigar box for money, a pitcher of Kool-Aid, and a pack of paper cups, next to a construction site, figuring that I'd get a lot of business from the thirsty workers, but it was right across the street from the Tastee Diner, so the competition drove me out of business.

Once, when I was toying with the idea of becoming a doctor when I grew up, Carolyn made me give her a shot of B-12 vitamins, bending over so I could slap her bare rump and plunge in the long syringe. I was elated that the injection was successful, but my career goal changed overnight. I never again entertained the idea of attending medical school.

Carolyn herself wished that she had studied medicine and liked to diagnose cases and prescribe medications—or at least tell ailing people what to take. When she was studying voice at the Peabody Conservatory, she hung around with medical students at Johns Hopkins when they dissected cadavers. "I had them save goodies for me," she said, "like an ear or a bony finger that I'd attach to a door knob." She claimed to have delivered a baby on pages of the Baltimore *Sun*. "Always use fresh newspapers," she declared. "Don't use towels, my darling. Newsprint is sterile."

She used the spare bedroom as her voice studio. One day, I was reading on the closed-up sofabed while she was giving a lesson to a young baritone named Ed. While he was in the middle of a song, I got up and left the room, reading my book as I walked away. After he had gone, Carolyn was furious.

"You should have seen the look on his face!" she said, "His voice fell. He was crestfallen that you didn't stay to hear him sing. He was singing for you! Nothing makes me madder than a lack of empathy. You have to put yourself in another person's place. How would you feel if someone walked out when you were performing?" Carolyn tried to make it up to Ed by letting him use the studio so he could sleep with a woman he was dating, but she never forgave him for leaving bloody sheets on the folded-out sofa-bed.

Carolyn's other students included several of the Singing Sergeants from the Air Force Band and members of the road company of *My Fair Lady*, which was then on a run at the National Theatre. A student named Bill gave me clarinet lessons, and another named Mark gave me a job at his piano repair shop when I was 18. The most musically successful of her original students was Kermit Finstad, a tall Nordic baritone with a big smile and an impressive crop of blond hair. When Carolyn was the vocal director of Menotti's *Amahl and the Night Visitors* at American University, Kermit sang the role of Melchior. He went on to teach voice and conduct choirs at Gettysburg College—and kept in touch with Carolyn and my mother for the rest of their lives.

But Carolyn needed money, so she decided to find another place for her voice studio and rented the extra bedroom to boarders. Two of them lived there in quick succession, both German men assigned temporarily to Washington, D.C., the first named Wilhelm and the second Wolfgang. When I was struggling with Geography in seventh grade, I decided to choose Germany as the subject for the nation booklet I was supposed to assemble. I thought I could get help from Wilhelm, who had accompanied the three of us to Christmas dinner at Aunt Sarah's house. He might have helped, but I procrastinated so much that I missed the deadline and had to write the report after he had moved out of the apartment.

Wolfgang was attracted to Carolyn, who was still gorgeous, buxom, and a shameless flirt, like my mother. He made it clear that he wanted to go to bed with her, so she told him to go to the drug store and buy a pack of condoms, which she always pronounced "cundums." When he got back, she told him, "Now, I want you to take this pair of scissors, march yourself to the bathroom, cut each one of those things in half, and flush them down the toilet. That's where your mind's been, and that's where they're going." I heard the story from both Carolyn and my mother. It was clear that Wolfgang, who had purchased a jumbo box of assorted condoms, never again brought up the subject of sex.

He left soon afterwards, and Carolyn gave up on taking in boarders. She moved her studio back from the basement of St. John's Episcopal Church, where I rehearsed with the choir when I was a boy soprano. The organist and choir director, John Spaulding, paid his choristers, so I actually got money for my singing. I loved getting out of Sunday school early so I could put on the cassock and cotta and march in the processional. I liked the hymns so much I recognized them by their numbers in the hymnal—and for Christmas, one year, my mother gave me a copy with my name engraved in gold on the red cover. I liked the chants, the anthems, the Doxology, and the recessionals. I liked evensong services, even though they conflicted with football games on television. There was a "certain slant of light" through the tall windows that I recalled when I first read the Emily Dickinson poem, a certain quietness that I might not have been able to appreciate and savor if I had not been sitting on a pew in the choir stall.

When we sang "Come unto Him" from Handel's *Messiah*, the whole group of boy sopranos blending together instead of a soloist, I tried to sound like a grown-up singer with a full, rich voice—like Carolyn, really—not with the sweet, clear timbre of a boy. She gave me a couple of voice lessons, telling me to stand up straight and stop slouching, to open my mouth wider, to sing from the diaphragm and not through my nose, to support the sound, to *think* a pitch before trying to sing it, not to raise my head when I sang a higher note because that would affect my throat, and to keep the tone "pure, pure, pure." When I started to sing a piece, she interrupted constantly to correct the mistakes I made, telling me I had to break bad habits instead of perpetuating them.

Now and then, she produced a long, low note to demonstrate how it should be done, and I was amazed by the power and beauty of her voice, even after she had given up singing professionally. John Spaulding let her use the choir room to give voice lessons—and would do so again when she needed the space—but he really wanted to hire her as his soprano soloist. I'm not sure why she rebuffed his offers. Maybe it was too much of a comedown from the heights she had known, or maybe she was too afraid to attempt a comeback after so many years away from the stage.

The three of us still did a lot of things together. They took me to movies not intended for children, such as *Fanny*, and I was titillated by a scene in which the mother finds a boy's belt in her daughter's bedroom and says something like "Now you'll *have* to get married!" When they took me to see *Auntie Mame*, I couldn't believe how much Carolyn resembled the flamboyant star, Rosalind Russell. As we left the theatre, she told me, "My darling, I'm *your* Auntie Mame."

We liked going downtown to O'Donnell's Seafood Restaurant, where Carolyn ordered a Gibson and my mother an Old Fashioned. When I complained that my Shirley Temple was a cocktail for little girls, they reassured me, "You can call it a Roy Rogers." We ate crab Norfolk, sautéed in butter and served in the sizzling skillet. I loved to look at the porthole in the wall next to the padded booth where we sat. Behind the round pane of glass, a cardboard sheet of green waves moved back and forth beneath a blue sky. It felt as though we were on a ship, rolling on the ocean. I found out, years later, that one of my mother's regrets was that she had sold her most precious ring in that restaurant. Did she do it to get back at Carolyn? Or to placate her by divesting herself of a band her former husband had put on her finger? Or to smash the memory of her own mother by disposing of one of her bequests? Or to show off, demonstrating that nothing from the past, not even gold or diamonds, mattered as much as her love for Carolyn? The only thing I know for sure is that drunkenness was involved.

My mother loved going to parties, which Carolyn often avoided. She became vivacious and effervescent, losing her inhibitions, her face more florid and animated after she had drunk her first cocktail and smoked a few Kents. If there was a piano in the vicinity, she claimed the bench and started playing in her high-spirited, bouncy style, specializing in swing versions of tunes like "Stardust," even though Carolyn had told her she "always got the chords wrong." Her favorite piece, which she had learned by ear, was called "Near You" and featured a boogie-woogie bass part for the left hand.

Bobby and Carolyn reminded me of Lucille Ball and Vivian Vance on television, female buddies who happened to be raising a child together, whether or not they lived in the same apartment. I rationalized their relationship in terms of comedy. When the emotional weather became too tempestuous and they lost control of their passions, they could retreat to separate residences.

Disclosure #7

Carolyn and my mother attended only one meeting of the P.T.A. at Bethesda Elementary, and now and then they laughed about the experience, sharing the joke with each other, but not with me.

I assume they were embarrassed to show up together, as a couple, as I was embarrassed whenever I sat in class and had to fill out an information form that had spaces for "Mother" and "Father" but just one address for both, no allowances or blanks to fill in for divorced parents or significant cousins.

Aria in the State Mental Hospital

1.

When I was nine, my mother and I attended Carolyn Long's last public concert, in which she was the soprano soloist in an all-Bach program at Constitution Hall on April 10, 1960. The conductor, George Manos, lived down the hall from our apartment. He was the founder of the Oratorio Society of Washington, and this concert was its first performance. He went on to direct the National Gallery Orchestra and write a memoir, *The President's Pianist.*

Carolyn's career was on hiatus, at best, but she was still in some demand, at least locally. Karl Halvorson persuaded her to participate as soprano soloist in services at All Souls Unitarian Church. But the only big invitation that came her way was the first performance by the newly formed Oratorio Society.

Carolyn was friends with important people in the classical music scene in Washington, D.C., in the early 1960s. When she threw a party, she invited luminaries like Paul Hume, the music critic of the Washington *Post,* Paul Callaway, the organist of the National Cathedral, and Todd Duncan, the original Porgy in George Gershwin's *Porgy and Bess,* and they all showed up. Because she had performed over a hundred concerts on the Gershwin Festival tour led by a young Lorin Maazel, she saw herself as a rival of Duncan, who also taught voice lessons in the area.

I liked to rummage through Carolyn's battered steamer trunk from her years on tour. It was full of concert programs, clippings from newspapers about her performances, glossy photographs, and other memorabilia from her singing career, all jumbled together. As I browsed through the material—what my mother would call "snooping"—I was especially impressed by an article that appeared in the Birmingham News in 1946 when Carolyn was the soprano soloist with the Straus Festival. The "drama, music, radio editor" declared that if Carolyn Long "isn't grabbed off by some movie studio when she sings with the Festival in California this season—then I'll quit predicting." She called Carolyn "stunning... a beautiful girl with a personality as warm and radiant as her lyric soprano voice." She was convinced that "a brilliant future lies ahead." At the end of the long, gushing article, she bet that people "would soon be hearing that fresh young soprano voice of hers—free and clear in the high notes, rich and warm in the lower register—in some of the new musical pictures that are to be made in Hollywood this year, a year that will find classical and semi-classical crowding out jive and jitterbug." Like so many other people who saw and heard Carolyn, including my mother, the reviewer was smitten. Her criticism was really a love note.

Carolyn was frank about sex, up to a point. She claimed that she taught me about the birds and the bees because my mother and father wouldn't do it. "I always made sure my accompanists were queer," she told me. "I didn't want them trying to get in bed with me when we were on tour." She kept in close touch with one of her pianists, Stanton Carter, who visited us several times, beginning when we lived in the one-bedroom apartment on Battery Lane. She called him "one of the boys" and prided herself on her knack for recognizing when people were gay. She warned Stan, in a joking way, to keep away from me, calling me "her boy."

Like my mother, Carolyn had an appetite for fun, and it often came from doing something wicked. "We were at a party after a concert," she said, "and I went up to Stan—I was still wearing one of my low-cut gowns—and I said, 'Stan, I'm going to rape you.' He looked terrified, and I chased him around the piano, around the whole house, from room to room, and then, when I finally cornered him, ha! He threw up on me, all over my beautiful gown."

Carolyn was educating me. She let me taste her wine, saying "In Italy, they wean children on it. It's part of every meal." She taught me the word "claque," saying that in Italy they paid people to attend an opera and cheer wildly for their favorite singer and whistle derisively at others. At any point, since spontaneity was one of her guiding principles, she might start singing a scatological ditty:

> Oh, she ripped and she roared,
> And she done it on the floor,
> And she wiped herself
> On the knob of the door!

She told me, "Darling, if you ever have any questions about sex, just ask me." I was so embarrassed by the prospect, I never did.

She was generous with stories about her singing career. Nothing kept her from a concert. When the car that was transporting Carolyn and her accompanist broke down in Texas, she hired an ambulance. When there was no way to drive over the snowy roads in Newfoundland, she hired a dogsled. When her airplane had to make a crash landing in Idaho, she led the passengers in singing to keep up their spirits and managed to get to the concert hall, but she didn't have time to change her clothes so she brought her luggage on stage, flung her fur coat on the grand piano, and started singing an Italian air.

"There was a burial at sea when I was crossing the Atlantic," she said. "I was in bed with the captain, both of us naked. We were toasting each other with champagne, and I had the funeral wreath on my head."

She gave several concerts with Mario Lanza and talked about cutting his hair, trimming his pompadour. She intimated that they had been lovers. The proof was an autographed glossy photo he'd inscribed:

> I love you
> I love you
> I love you
> What the hell else could I possibly say?
> Christ! your terrific
>
> Mario Lanza

She attracted admirers everywhere. After singing at the White House, she danced with the elderly Vice President, Alben Barkley, who was hosting the dinner for President Truman, and when they were finished he pinched her ass.

She made only one record album, singing a small but impressive role in Arthur Honegger's *Jeanne d'Arc au bûcher*, conducted by Eugene Ormandy, who was so grateful to her for dubbing in another singer's part that he gave her his baton. When Carolyn directed a variety show at the state mental hospital, just outside our hometown, she presented it to a patient who conducted an invisible orchestra while an overture blared from a phonograph.

The afternoon concert in Constitution Hall went on for nearly three hours, moving from one cantata to the next, and then to the familiar Orchestral Suite in D, until it concluded with Bach's *Magnificat*. At home, I had been exposed to a lot of classical music, and I liked it, but the opening chorale really grabbed me, and I found it more memorable than the best movie sound track. I can still remember how Carolyn sang "Quia respexit humilitatem," her thrilling voice and powerful delivery hitting me with a visceral punch. She stood "like a captain on the poop deck," as she described it to me later, in front of the other soloists and the orchestra, gorgeous as a movie star in one of her concert gowns, a black one, all of which would later be stolen from the back of my mother's Rambler American.

The reviews were favorable. In the Washington *Post*, Robert Evett praised the "very beautiful singing" of the soloists, noting that Carolyn, as well as two of the others, "sang with great authority, but in a style which is perhaps a little too operatic for this music." In the *Evening Star*, Irving Lowens wrote that "the afternoon's soloists, all of whom had plenty to do, proved first-rate. The two local artists, Carolyn Long and Rilla Mervine, held their own very well with the Messrs. [Charles] Bressler and [Ara] Berberian, who are featured with the New York Pro Musica and the Shaw Chorale, respectively." Lowens complained that the conductor's tempi for the arias "were so unconscionably slow and stately that, with lesser soloists, there would have been a real disaster."

The Latin text of Carolyn's aria meant "He has looked with great favor on his lowly servant," words spoken by the Virgin Mary. But my mother could have easily substituted feminine for masculine pronouns to make it personal between the two of them: *She has looked with great favor on her lowly servant.* She was in a state of nervous excitement and exultation during the concert, clutching my wrist several times, and I know she felt grateful that Carolyn, the great singer, had looked down on her with love. Hero-worship, a fan's devotion, was one source of her infatuation and attachment. Later, when they went through personal, medical, financial, or romantic difficulties, my mother liked to affirm her commitment to Carolyn by telling me, "I know what she was."

2.

In the spring of 1986, my mother donated Carolyn Long's press clippings, programs, and other papers to the Peabody Conservatory. Both the director and the archivist wrote a series of grateful acknowledgments to Carolyn and my mother, praising the "marvelous job assembling them" and calling them "a splendid addition to our collection." They referred to my mother as Carolyn's cousin, but an article in the *Peabody News* altered the relationship, saying that the "Long Papers were lovingly assembled by her close friend, Carolyn B. Drury."

It reminds me of the time I sent clippings of my classical music reviews from the college newspaper at Stony Brook University to Paul Hume, in the hope of getting a summer internship at the Washington *Post*. He sent me a long, kind, detailed reply, telling me that none was available, referring to Carolyn several times as my cousin. My mother made photocopies and mailed them to everyone she knew, but she carefully inked out every reference to Carolyn as our "cousin."

She preserved, in two oversized binders, copies of press clippings donated to Peabody. Her own reward lay in curating and chronicling the proof of Carolyn's accomplishments. In notes I found after her death, my mother wrote, "Anything I did to help her justified my existence." That included taking care of her when her health failed, joining their finances together, spending as much time with her as she could, hiring sitters when she couldn't, and promoting Carolyn's career, keeping the memory alive by assembling her press clippings, gathering what recordings she could find on 78s, tapes, and wire recordings and transferring them to cassettes. She campaigned for Carolyn to get some sort of tangible recognition for her singing career. She supplied the materials for the Cambridge *Daily Banner* to print a full-page article on Carolyn. She lobbied for the county to name the new bridge to Hooper's Island after Carolyn, although officials resisted the appeal.

The press clippings contradicted some of the errors that had crept into Carolyn's teaching résumé. She claimed to have starred in the original performance of Gian Carlo Menotti's *The Old Maid and the Thief,* but her clippings show that she sang the role of Laetitia in the local premiere, which took place in Baltimore on April 17, 1943. The opera was also performed in front of an audience of 1,500 sailors at the Bainbridge Naval Station a month later: "When Carolyn Long, as the pretty maid, walked on the stage, the sailors unleashed blasts of whistling, stomped and applauded."

After she signed a contract with Columbia Artists Management, an excerpt from an early review appeared in her promotional materials:

> Hers is a voice of warm and brilliant quality, resonance, and rich in its overtones, through which is achieved that tone color that gives dramatic significance to songs. The result is a happy and rare combination of a sensitive appreciation of the melodic line, clear perspective of tone color and limpid beauty of tone.

During that matinee recital in St. Louis in February 1941, Carolyn sang "Deh vieni, non tardar" from Mozart's *The Marriage of Figaro*, "Depuis le jour" from Charpentier's *Louise*, and "Pace, pace, mio Dio" from Verdi's *La Forza del Destino*, all pieces that remained in her concert repertoire throughout her career.

In the fall of 1946, she embarked on her first long tour, appearing as the soprano soloist for the Straus Festival in nearly 50 cities. President Truman attended the performance in Constitution Hall. The Atlanta *Constitution* reported that the audience was cold through the first half of the program there, and it was "not until lovely Carolyn Long, soprano, sang the beautiful 'My Hero' that the music lovers warmed up and applauded in the traditional Atlanta manner." My mother liked to laugh about the typographical error that appeared in a review from the New Orleans *States*: "Distinguished by a voice of wide range and a tonal quality of warmth and richness, Miss Long sank with emotional expression."

Reviewers, male and female, were wowed by Carolyn's stunning good looks. In Houston, she was "a curvaceous warm throated soprano." In Phoenix, she was "a mature brunette with beauty and winsome dimples and a figure like a goddess," who was "startling in a Kelly green satin gown, extremely low cut and strapless, which clung tight to her beautiful form." That's about as close to pornography as any classical music review got in the 1940s.

In June 1947, Carolyn sang with Mario Lanza in New Orleans. During their three concerts, they performed several duets, including "O soave fanciulla" from Puccini's *La Bohème* and two songs from operettas by Sigmund Romberg, but music critics complained about the public address system, saying that "unfortunately, except for a few brief passages, the microphone distortion resulted in a battle of voices." On the second night, a reviewer noted that "Unlike Mr. Lanza, Miss Long revealed much improvement last night, but she also excelled more in the operetta selections than in 'Voi lo sapete' from Mascagni's *Cavalleria Rusticana*."

Carolyn spent the summer of 1948 singing in many operas produced at the Cincinnati Zoo under the aegis of the Metropolitan Opera. In Gounod's *Faust*, she played the "pants role" of Siébel. One of the local newspapers printed a photograph of Ezio Pinza, who played Mephistopheles, shaking hands with Carolyn, both in costume. Her parts were minor: Herodias's page in *Salome*, Countess Ceprano and Giovanna in *Rigoletto*, Kate Pinkerton in *Madame Butterfly*, Gianettina in *L'Elisire d'Amore*, a "lusty and lyrical shepherd" in *Tannhäuser*, Flora in *La Traviata*, the Priestess in *Aida*, Inez in *Il Trovatore*, and Frasquita in *Carmen*. She had already performed several of these roles at the San Antonio Opera Festival the year before.

The critic of the Cincinnati *Enquirer* noted that, in Richard Strauss's *Salome*, "Carolyn Long was a lovely page, whose freshness contrasted with the psychopathic shouting of the others. Stage direction, however, should have kept her in the background, rather than permitting her ever to mount the palace steps and dwarf the figure of Salome." Not that she was tall—her press releases announced that she was 5'5" and weighed 125 pounds. Another reviewer said, of her performance in Gounod's *Faust*, "Never have I heard the role of Siébel sung so well. Carolyn Long is to be congratulated on the warmth of her voice and the intelligence of her portrayal." In Wagner's *Tannhäuser*, she was a "welcome newcomer who is learning fast." As the priestess in Verdi's *Aida*, she "was authoritative, if a little earthy, considering the mystic ceremony in which she was heard." In his review of Bizet's *Carmen*, a critic wrote, "One of the most ingenious singers this season, Carolyn Long has taken over a dozen roles and made them her own, without having appeared previously on the professional operatic stage. Her latest and most attractive part was Frasquita last night, sung with ease and freshness." Of her later performance in the same role, the same critic praised her "innate intelligence" and "comprehension born of study." The season was a triumph for Carolyn, but she still had to figure out how to advance to leading roles.

The press clippings covered her private life too. After her divorce from Hugh Blair Grigsby Long, Carolyn married Henry C. "Duke" Duffield, Jr., on March 8, 1949, in Elkton, Maryland. He was a real cowboy who had ridden in the Calgary Stampede and other rodeos. He attended her concert in Walsenburg, Colorado, near his Journey's End Ranch, and then followed her tour around the country until she agreed to his proposal of marriage. "Miss Long used to hate cowboy songs," the Vancouver *Daily Province* reported, "but Mr. Duffield sings them to her and now she's crazy about them." Both marriages ended in divorce with petitions filed against Carolyn for "desertion."

She often boasted that she had sung in the White House, but that wasn't quite accurate, since it was then under repair. However, she did perform at a dinner for President Truman, hosted by Vice President Alben Barkley at the Carlton Hotel on May 31, 1949. She claimed that the Vice President pinched her in the rear after they danced, but a newspaper article said that he "couldn't let the evening pass without kissing [her]."

There weren't any reviews of Carolyn's radio appearances, but a number of newspaper articles announced them. She sang "Mi chiamano Mimi" from *La Bohème* on the Harvest of Stars radio broadcast hosted by actor Raymond Massey on July 30, 1946. During another episode of the program, on July 16, 1950, Carolyn and tenor James Melton sang a duet, Jerome Kern's "They Didn't Believe Me" from *The Girl from Utah*. A recording of the broadcast survives, and her voice sounds thrilling. During the bantering before their duet, she also speaks Italian—and that was before she had lived in Italy.

In the summer of 1949, Carolyn again took to the stage outdoors, starring in two operettas in Vancouver. As Evalina in *Bloomer Girl*, she "sang excellently." Another review praised her "fine performance and magnificent voice." As Edvard Grieg's sweetheart in *Song of Norway*, she gave "a superb performance as a singer and actress. Hers is a most appealing voice, rich and full of warmth."

Most of Carolyn's performances, numbering in the hundreds, were solo recitals accompanied by a pianist, part of the Community Concert series that brought classical music to towns all over the country, many of them out-of-the-way places. When she joked about the "Pee-Pot Circuit," she was referring to Johnstown, Pottstown, and Chambersburg in Pennsylvania.

Her programs were eclectic and multilingual. A typical program began with something old, such as "Nymphs and Shepherds" by Purcell, and then proceeded to *chansons*, such as Poulenc's "C'est le joli printemps," and then to arias, such as Puccini's "Vissi d'arte, vissi d'amore," and then to Lieder, such as Hugo Wolf's "Im Frühling," and then to spirituals, such as "Steal Away." She made a point of performing songs written by women, including "Think on Me" by Alicia Scott and a number of songs by her friend Margaret Carreau.

The earliest clipping from the Community Concert series dates from

1946, when Carolyn sang at a junior high school auditorium in Bayonne, New Jersey. The reviewer begins by lavishing praise on her singing as well as her beauty, pointing out her "skill of holding her audience and feeling at home with them" and quoting a member of the audience who called her "the sweetest singer I have heard in years."

On stage, Carolyn had "that elusive thing called personality," a reviewer in Corinth, Mississippi, observed. He praised the "spontaneous, heart-felt quality" of her singing and summed up what made her so successful as a lyric soprano:

> Miss Long's voice is a beautiful one of considerable range, quite even, warm and eloquent. She employs it with unerring musicianship, a happy combination which, unfortunately, does not always exist. Each song was projected with a vivid sense of dramatic conduct as well as sheer delight in melodic line. And all this with excellent diction in three languages. She is a singer who is mistress of many nuances as well as of the broader contrasts.... Consider, for example, the exquisite French songs such as the silvery "Chanson triste" of Duparc and the heavy dramatics of the "Pace, pace" of Verdi. The latter, indeed, is from the standard repertoire of the dramatic soprano. Here, and at other times, Miss Long's voice took on an added depth and richness not usually associated with the lyric voice.... Or again, consider the contrast between a bewitching song like Ravel's "Tout gai" and the religious awe of the spiritual, "Were You There." The point is that Miss Long seems at home anywhere along the gamut. She makes each song unique.

Carolyn liked to introduce her songs and give the audience "interesting footnotes" and stories about her career. At a concert in Newfoundland (where she once reached an auditorium by dogsled), she recalled having trouble finding transportation when she was scheduled to give a concert in the hills of Arkansas. She called a funeral parlor to ask about renting a hearse, and the mortician sounded so "sepulchral," she exclaimed, "Cheer up! We're alive." At another recital, she introduced "Linstead Market" by explaining that she learned it from a Jamaican taxicab driver "at her own expense," since he kept the meter running.

Instead of acting aloof, she tried to break down the distance between herself and her listeners, having a gift for "making each one in the audience feel that she is singing especially for him." In Tucumcari, New Mexico, she asked for the house lights to be left on "so she could see her listeners and feel their friendliness." In Great Bend, Kansas, she said that if the lights were not turned on, "I'd rather stay home and sing in my own bathroom. When I can't see their faces, and they can't read their programs, what good is it?" In Newfoundland, she accompanied herself on piano and led the audience in singing "Ode to Newfoundland." She thrived on spending time with people who loved music. "I came from an unmusical town," she told an audience in Newport News. "I was the first singer to emerge there and they thought I was peculiar."

Carolyn took every opportunity, however, to depart from her exhausting schedule of recitals if she could perform with orchestras. In 1951, she was the soprano soloist for the Verdi *Requiem* in Houston, where the *Chronicle* reported that she sang "with impressive purity and roundness of tone, at all volumes and right through the scale."

Later that year in Austin, she starred as Tosca in a concert version of Puccini's opera conducted by Ezra Rachlin. One reviewer called her "the hit of the program" and declared that "this lady is destined to become an artist of the very first order." He also quoted Carolyn: "It takes the strength of a bucking bronco to carry on this program I have set for myself, but I haven't been bucked off yet!" Another reviewer called the production a "top-grade performance sparked by Carolyn Long in the title role" and went on to say that "Miss Long, a warm, attractive Tosca, sang with expressive feeling and a natural flair for stage work."

After singing the role of Micaela in a concert version of *Carmen* with the Tulsa Philharmonic, she must have felt she was on her way to the leading roles she wanted. A reviewer said that her "beautiful voice, destined to take its owner far on the road to success, was handled with artistic mastery, especially as it is naturally somewhat heavier than that usually chosen for the role of Micaela, but its range and flexibility resulted in a performance that was outstanding."

No single performance in Carolyn's career received more reviews than a production of Arthur Honegger's *Jeanne d'Arc au bûcher* on November 18, 1952, in Carnegie Hall in New York, with Eugene Ormandy conducting the Philadelphia Orchestra and Carolyn in the role of Marguerite. Virgil Thomson praised the "fine singing cast" but devoted most of his review to lambasting the composition, which he considered "pretentious, second-rate, and in large measure second-hand." Olin Downes, however, found the dramatic oratorio a "work of profound feeling as well as dramatic power" and praised the soloists for their mastery "not only of singing but of superb French diction." Soon afterwards, the work was recorded and issued as a two-disc set on Columbia Records.

The highlight of Carolyn's singing career was certainly her year as the soprano soloist in the Gershwin Festival tour led by a young Lorin Maazel. An article in the Duluth *News-Tribune* called her the "Gershwin Girl." Supposedly Ira Gershwin, the composer's brother and collaborator who was a consultant for the tour, had chosen Carolyn personally.

She was paired with baritone Theodor Uppman, who had originated the title role in Benjamin Britten's *Billy Budd*, and their "voices blended beautifully." A reviewer in Huntington, West Virginia, thought that they "could hardly have been improved upon in their assignment to provide charm and variety." Their duets included "Bess, You Is My Woman Now," "Embraceable You," "Soon," "Of Thee I Sing," and "'S Wonderful." A critic in Cedar Rapids complained that their "hand-hold, arm-around-waist, stage business might have been a bit overdone. But since it did not detract much from the performance and since the audience seemed to like it, perhaps the action was justified."

A critic in Brunswick, Georgia, called Carolyn "the beautiful, heart-warming soprano" and "the girl one can't forget," asserting that the soloists "were so perfectly teamed that the audience was sixteen again, listening to Jeanette McDonald [sic] and Nelson Eddy. But the voices of Uppman and Long can go places where McDonald and Eddy never had a look-in."

In her solos, Carolyn managed her rich soprano with "fine musical intelligence," especially the "wonderful primitive effect she got in the cadenza" at the end of "My Man's Gone Now." A critic in Lewiston, Idaho, raved about her "chillingly dramatic glissando into the high register, punctuating this song of grief." Her other solo was "The Man I Love."

Carolyn's voice was praised as "glorious," "clear and sweet," "pretty," "lovely," "thrilling," "warmly soaring," "smooth and luscious," "pure and crystal-clear," "strictly feminine, firm, and remarkably expressive." She was "an audience favorite from the moment when she first entered, smilingly and with great poise." In Colorado Springs, she had "some melting high notes which are especially effective, and a charming, winning personality."

In a letter to Carolyn in 1983, Ted Uppman wrote:

> I think of you often, Carolyn, dear friend, and your beautiful voice and presence. In my travels around the country, and in Canada, I still meet people who remember, with joy, our performances, as well as your lovely solo recitals & appearances with orchestras.
>
> It's hard to believe, sometimes, that Lorin Maazel, whom we had to teach how to conduct singers, is now General Director of the Vienna State Opera. We should be getting a commission for having taught him so well.

Reviewing a Gershwin concert in 1954, Olin Downes, the music critic of the New York *Times*, pointed out that the "singing was excellent, especially that of Carolyn Long, who sustained her melodic line beautifully and sang with a spirit and an élan that matched her technical mastery and the sensuous appeal of her voice."

Carolyn wrote him a letter, asking for advice about her career, and he replied, saying that she had impressed him as "a real artist... one with the native sensibility and capacity for self-expression and communication in song which is even more essential to an artist's success than the fine qualities of voice which you have." He also approved of her intention "to study longer and carefully in the direction of opera," which he considered a "very natural field" for her.

A column in the Battle Creek *Enquirer and News* suggested that Carolyn was preparing to take a gamble with her career. Someone asked, "Why is she not singing at the 'Met'?" The columnist reported that she was "likely to be singing at the 'Met' next season. She will not accept the invitation until she has mastered more leading roles, as she does not intend to sing minor parts."

In a gossip column in 1954, *Musical Courier* reported that Carolyn "has done what very few people have the courage to do. She is interrupting a lucrative career to study opera for one year in Italy. She feels it necessary, and that the gamble will be worth it. Feels she can't go along forever without branching out... kept too busy on the road for Columbia the last five years. She says that it's now or never, and she wouldn't be able to take the time and concentrate here. Gossip says it's a really fine soprano voice with a particular leaning toward Puccini and Verdi..."

There was a scattering of concerts in 1954 before Carolyn departed for her sabbatical in Italy. In January, she and Theodor Uppman sang together in a concert devoted to the songs of Rodgers and Hammerstein in Constitution Hall. In March, she sang the role of Marguerite in Berlioz's *The Damnation of Faust* in Baltimore. A reviewer observed that she had "an even scale, and she produced full tones of agreeable quality, though with a vibrato too pronounced—not wide but rapid."

She was the soprano soloist with the Tulsa Philharmonic when they performed the choral fourth movement of Beethoven's Ninth Symphony. In the first half of the program, which was devoted to Mozart, she sang "Dove sono" from *The Marriage of Figaro* and the duet "Là ci darem la mano" from *Don Giovanni*, two pieces that suggest potential for future work she might have pursued.

After she had spent nearly two years in Italy, a long article in the Cambridge *Daily Banner* celebrated her return. The headline claimed that she had "eight operas to her credit," but those were apparently parts she studied, not roles she performed. Although she was "selected to sing in the Teatra Reggia in Parma," it did not say she actually appeared on stage there. The only performing it mentioned was Carolyn rehearsing in her studio in Milan, crowds gathering outside to listen and applaud, crying "Encore! Encore!" There were clues to Carolyn's desperate state of mind throughout the article, which talked about the poverty and hunger she found in Italy. A "rest period" was now more important than a contract. Her "depression" was slight compared to what others around her were suffering. The passive voice crept into the account, as if unfortunate things were simply happening to Carolyn. Operas "were to be learned." Time had to be "allotted for lessons." A fall on the marble floor in her apartment resulted in a broken arm.

The article included a photograph of Carolyn on the Queen Frederica, standing with her elbow on the ship's railing, next to a life preserver, smiling, and yet her moon face looked tired, wan, swollen, like the carefully made-up mask of a worn-out courtesan, even though she was trying to look brave and confident.

Only a few clippings remain after that, most impressively the reviews from the major Washington dailies after her performance in Bach's *Magnificat* at Constitution Hall, the concert my mother and I attended. The last clipping is Paul Hume's column, "Postlude," dated February 2, 1967, in which the music critic recalled that Carolyn was one of the soloists in *Jeanne d'Arc au bûcher* and gave a plug for Carolyn's voice studio in Bethesda.

Some reviews of Carolyn's performances eluded the clipping service employed by Columbia Artists. Browsing through microfilm, I found a column about a talent show directed by Carolyn in 1958 at the state mental hospital, just east of Cambridge, Maryland, on the site now occupied by the Hyatt Regency Chesapeake Bay Resort. I already knew the story of how she presented a baton, a gift from Eugene Ormandy, to an elderly patient who conducted an imaginary orchestra while a record played. But I learned that the program also featured a Hawaiian dance, a patient playing rock and roll on a mouth harp, the recitation of several poems, and a puppet show with Indians, clowns, and Chinese dancers. "When the program had come to a close," the column reported, "a young lady stepped to the microphone and requested that Miss Long sing two numbers, and she did." The article did not specify what the songs were, but it did mention that the piano accompanist was "Mrs. Philip Drury," my mother. The two of them had recorded their practice sessions for "Vittoria, vittoria, mio core," a seventeenth-century aria by Giacomo Carissimi, on a wire recorder, and my mother later had the spools transferred to cassette. Listening to their collaboration always gives me a jolt of happiness hopelessly tangled up with grief. The song brings back those final months in 1958 before my father left for New York and my mother and Carolyn took me on a trek toward Austin, Texas, where some mirage of a music job was supposedly waiting for the glamorous soprano.

Defeat was close by, coming to the surface when an ad in the *Daily Banner* that same week announced *Seven Hills of Rome*, a new film starring Mario Lanza, Carolyn's old singing partner and paramour, the movie poster proclaiming "HE'S BACK...BETTER THAN EVER" and crowing "LANZA SINGS TO A GORGEOUS NEW GIRL!" Carolyn was back in her hometown, after hard times in Italy and a nervous breakdown, but she wasn't better than ever. For one night, though, in front of a packed house, not all of the audience members insane, my mother and Carolyn performed together in what amounted to her last song recital, the victory in their hearts not just part of the Italian lyrics Carolyn sang so thrillingly.

Disclosure #8

At the time of Carolyn's performance in Bach's **Magnificat** in Constitution Hall, my mother was friends with the conductor's brother Andy, an automobile salesman who talked her into buying a Rambler American station wagon and later a red Hornet. "I really got stung," she liked to say, but she still remained friends with Andy, whom I remember as a round-faced, chubby, smiling man with thick eyebrows, not dignified and distinguished like his brother the conductor. He also talked my mother into posing for a newspaper ad for the dealership, and my mother thought it was the best photograph ever taken of her. But the quotations in the ad were entirely fabricated:

"EVERYTHING WORKS—
NOTHING RATTLES!"

Carolyn B. Drury, Bethesda bank clerk: "I thought all wagons were trucks until I drove a Cranston Rambler. Even with the children and the dog, we all have loads of space. And all this for about $1000 less than we might have paid."

We thought it was funny that she claimed to have children (plural) and a dog. But the portrait is fetching. She's standing against a brick wall, wearing a sleeveless summer blouse with a flared collar, looking to her right with a big smile that showed off the bright red lipstick she wore, prominent even in black and white. Her hair, still black, is perfect, for once, short but full and luxuriant on top. It's a study in curves, her oval face within the bigger oval delineated by her seemingly sculpted hair, with just the contrasting dip of a curly lock at the crown of her forehead. For once, the long nose she joked was "aristocratic" didn't stand out. Looking at the picture she considered her favorite likeness, I'm struck by how much she resembles Carolyn Long.

Side by side, they didn't look that much alike, my mother pretty, slim at the time, almost delicate and doll-like, Carolyn buxom, flamboyant, and vivacious. But both were brown-eyed brunettes who wore their hair short and wavy, Carolyn's naturally curly, my mother's not. In pictures taken when they first started living together, Carolyn looks tough, with a wicked slant to her eyebrows, which she had to pencil in because her real ones were so faint. "She was beautiful," my mother said years later, "but it wasn't a natural beauty." My mother in those early pictures looks meek and vulnerable, a damsel in distress who's just been rescued, *an ingénue in a sappy movie from the 1930s. It's easy to tell who looks dominant, who subservient. But it was trickier than that. My mother did serve Carolyn, but she was also the one in charge, the one who fixed things, rewiring broken lamps and re-gilding the pier mirror, the one who ultimately made the decisions. She may have looked like the baby, but she did the babying.*

Beautiful Bobby from Downtown Bethesda

Like a minor-league baseball player working his way up through the farm system, my mother moved from one branch of the Bank of Bethesda to another, from Wildwood to Westwood, from the National Institutes of Health to Naval Medical Center. My favorite location was the drive-in branch, which reminded me of a submarine, its flat, overhanging roof like a ship's deck. Lanes ran in different directions on both sides of the long building, and I liked to ride my bicycle up to my mother's window and press on the long metal bar that rang a buzzer. Sometimes she gave me an advance on my allowance, putting bills and coins in an envelope and then placing it in the drawer that tilted open and extended to the outside. Sometimes she invited me in and introduced me to the young men she worked with. I especially liked Keith, who took me to a model railroad club in the Rockville train station, but she talked more about John Bowman, who didn't pay much attention to me.

One summer day, I was racing my bicycle against my friend Carla. I got to the bank first and glided down to my mother's window, which I approached too fast and too closely. I sliced the base of my left little finger on the bar you pressed to ring for the teller. Bone was showing.

"You almost cut off your finger," my mother said, another exaggeration she enjoyed repeating. "There was blood everywhere. No one was paying any attention to the customers. You created quite a commotion! I had to take you right to Suburban Hospital where they sewed it up."

She blossomed when she was promoted to the main branch, the triangular stone building at the intersection of Wisconsin Avenue and Old Georgetown Road. She was so friendly, gushing with the flirtatious charm of a Southern belle, customers lined up at her window. Her grumpiest regular was the CBS commentator Eric Sevareid. "He had a shrunken hand," she told me. But he always went to her window, even if he had to wait in line.

Through the connections she developed with her customers, she found summer jobs for me at the Chevy Chase Motor Lodge, where I worked as a bellhop, a Hot Shoppes drive-in restaurant, where I carried trays of food to people who sat in parked cars by lit-up menus, and an apartment complex where I worked on the grounds crew.

She made friends with everyone who worked there, from Luther and Joe, who served as couriers, to the president of the bank, George Sacks, with whom she developed a joking relationship. He often appeared on the balcony that overlooked the two-story lobby with its big windows, marble panels, and brass Art Deco fixtures and called down to her, "Drury, are you still working here?" She replied, "Why hello, Mister Sacks, you old goat. How's your love life?" He grumbled and went back to his office.

She put up a sign outside her window:

> Jesus saves.
> Why don't you?
> Bank of Bethesda
> gives 4.5% interest.

Mister Sacks made her take it down, worrying that it might offend people who were religious and thereby lose their business. What's shocking now, of course, is the amazingly high interest rate on a savings account.

She didn't like to follow rules. "Beautiful Bobby from downtown Bethesda!" is how she answered the phone at work. She was a ringleader when it came to mischief, organizing cocktail parties in the bank vault on Friday evenings after everyone had settled. When they ordered crabs from Bish Thompson's seafood restaurant, my mother insisted that they leave the crab shells there over the weekend, just for a joke. George Sacks didn't think it was funny that the vault stank when they opened it on Monday morning. "Drury," he said, "I know you're behind this. I could fire you!" But he didn't. Instead, when Cashell Shoemaker retired, Mister Sacks promoted my mother to head teller.

Cashell must have recommended her for the position. He was certainly smitten. "He was very kind to me," she said, "and his wife misinterpreted it. Poor old Cashell. He had a case on me." He even had a key to our apartment so he could run errands and deliver things she had requested. She called him one of her "lackeys."

It helped that she was an attractive woman who could manipulate a foolish old cashier. But my mother suffered from the prevalent bias against women in the work place. When a young man started working at the bank, he received higher pay than she did as head teller. She had every right to take legal action against the Bank of Bethesda.

But my mother didn't believe in litigation. When I was four or five, sitting on a branch of a tree, an older boy from across the street threw the inner tube from an automobile tire and knocked me down. I broke my right arm when I hit the ground, and Fredericka, the boy's mother, didn't talk to my mother for weeks because she was afraid that Bobby would take her to court and sue. My mother didn't take action against the bank, but it made her seethe as she struggled to pay her bills and raise me, so angry that eventually she quit.

Still, the job was also a source of pride, as well as fun. "I felt I was somebody there," she wrote in a note I found after her death. "I had tellers who worked under me, and they were my people. They looked up to me. I was responsible for them." In January 1970, they sent her a memorandum about "REHAB & RECREATION," which she preserved in her lockbox at home:

1. WELCOME BACK, WE ARE SO HAPPY TO HAVE YOU WITH US AGAIN.
2. WHILE YOU WERE GONE WE WORKED OURSELVES TO A FRAZZLE IN KEEPING WITH YOUR HIGH STANDARDS.
3. THEREFORE, IN VIEW OF THE ABOVE, WE FEEL AFTER SUCH A HARD TIME WE DESERVE A MUCH DESIRED "R&R."
4. STARTING MONDAY, WE ARE EACH TAKING A TWO (2) DAY HOLIDAY, STARTING WITH TELLER #1 THRU #5.

YOUR DEVOTED WORKERS

She had such a good time and put so much of herself into the job that she was worn out when she got home, even though the bank closed at three o'clock, except on Fridays, when they stayed open into the evening. She always took a nap after work.

When I visited her in the bank, she put up a "CLOSED" sign and took me around to visit the tellers who worked with her, as well as some of the auditors and bookkeepers who worked in the back. She took me into the cool vault, where she kept her cash drawer when she wasn't working, its huge, round, silvery door propped open. She showed me how she unstrapped the packets of fresh money that were sandwiched between bill-sized pieces of wood on which the currency left imprints, like capitalist Shrouds of Turin. She showed me how she could nudge an alarm with her knee if a robber tried to hold up the bank.

The tellers weren't supposed to sit in their cages when they waited on customers, but standing was hard for my mother because of her bad knees. So she got Joe to saw off several inches from the legs of a high wooden stool. She tied the cloth strings that were hanging from a cushion to the legs and leaned back against the stool, half sitting, half standing.

She arranged for Luther, Joe, or Cashell, even after his retirement, to pick her up in the morning and drive her home after work. One of the bookkeepers told her, "You're the only teller the bank provides with her own chauffeur."

"Nothing is dirtier than money," she told me. "After I've been handling bills, I need to wash my hands. I leave the bank every day with dirty hands." She worked in what she called a cage. Customers referred to it as her window.

When my father worked as a teller in Cambridge, he stood behind brass bars so he looked like a prisoner in jail, but my mother's cage in Bethesda had a counter but no bars. Bank tellers today call themselves Customer Service Representatives and work not in cages but at stations. "When they started bringing in computers," my mother said, "that's when I knew I had to get out."

It's interesting that she gravitated toward jobs that involved dealing with money in some way. When she was young, one of her summer jobs, besides defuzzing peaches, had been at the National Bank of Cambridge. Her husband had worked as a bank teller, so it made sense that she found the same kind of job after they separated. And when she left the bank, she worked as a bookkeeper, adding up credits and debits at Community Auto, a parts supply store.

Both of my parents were bank tellers, and there was one thing I promised myself. When I grew up, I'd never work in a bank.

My mother did find ways to augment her meager pay checks. People who still held gold currency sometimes brought in their coins and redeemed them at face value. They believed that an executive order by President Roosevelt in 1933 required them to turn in their gold to a Federal Reserve bank so it could be melted down and kept in reserve, probably in the form of bullion in Fort Knox, not realizing that collectors were exempt from this confiscation. Whenever a customer turned in a $2½ gold piece, my mother opened up her purse and put her own money, two worn bills and two quarters, in the till and kept the gold coin. She amassed a sizable collection that she enjoyed possessing for years and benefited from selling off, coin by coin, as her finances worsened. She left me several when she died, two of them hanging from gold necklaces, and they saved me from my own financial ruin, at least for a time. Her favorite was the rarest, a $20 gold coin, called a double eagle, designed by the sculptor Augustus St. Gaudens.

"There's a little larceny in all of us," she liked to say, and it's both shocking and not at all surprising that someone who worked with money would be attracted to it, interested in how to shave off her percentage of the proceeds and take her cut. She swiped a lot of things from the bank, including little blue zippered bags, marked with the bank's name in gold letters, that were perfect for her own letters and checkbooks. Once, when she'd been drinking, always a truth serum with her, she asked me, "Do you think I never took anything at the bank? I had ways so I wouldn't get caught, a little at a time. I just said that I'd come up short when I settled."

A long time after she quit, incensed when they wouldn't allow the head teller to take extra time off after an operation, she confided what she'd done in her teller's cage. "Every so often," she said, "I took a $20 bill from Earlene's cash drawer, never so much that she wouldn't think it was her own mistake when she came up short."

My mother was in her early forties then, her hair still dark, cut so it accentuated the long neck that Carolyn likened to a Modigliani, while Earlene looked older, her hair curled and dyed gray at the beauty parlor. Earlene was earnest and sober, an ideal foil for my mother's antics.

"Earlene did the Safeway deposits and there were a lot of them," my mother said. "She'd enter each one on the adding machine—*punch punch punch, punch punch punch*—but when she pressed 'TOTAL,' there was nothing. I'd put it on non-total. I was mean. But I was just having fun."

She considered stealing things a challenge, a chance to enjoy some risky fun. She was a careful, conservative thief. It began when she was ten—the year after her father died—and she stole a bugle, stuffing it in her coat. When her sister Sarah found out about her theft and tattled, their mother Sadie spanked Bobby with a silver brush.

She stole a book, *Red Howling Monkey*, from the Academy School, putting it in her book bag, but she burned it in the back yard. "I never enjoyed anything I stole," she told me when she was spending her last days in a nursing home, "because I always felt so guilty. Taking it was fun, a challenge. I should have had a school to teach people how to steal."

She stole Carolyn's "long favorite string of pearls" from Strawbridge & Clothier. I think she felt like Robin Hood, a virtuoso in her own right, a romantic scoundrel, justified in claiming a prize for her own Maid Marian. She stole a silver coffee pot from Billy's Carriage House in Georgetown, stuffing it in her big pocketbook. She couldn't even remember all the things she had stolen. I knew first-hand about the inflatable life-jacket she stole for me from the first airplane flight I ever took.

She was proudest of what was her final heist. After her sister Sarah died, she walked through her house while police were conducting an inventory of the property. My mother removed items she felt were rightfully hers, including a gold coin hanging from a gold necklace. "They never noticed anything missing," she said. "I only wish I'd taken more."

The only time anyone ever stopped her was in People's Drug Store on Arlington Road. They took her to a back room and searched her but found nothing. Luckily, it was one time when she *hadn't* pocketed something like a box of pills or a bottle of cologne. "We're not going to call the police," the manager told her, "but don't come back. Do your shopping elsewhere."

She usually stole things because someone had made her mad, like the rude waiter at Billy's Carriage House. I suppose that makes her a kleptomaniac, but I prefer to think of her pleasure and pride in thievery as part of her rebelliousness. "There's a little larceny in all of us," she repeated. "There was a lot in me."

Disclosure #9

My mother was supposed to be a boy, and she was interested in things that boys liked, especially tools. She liked to repair things all of her life, and always kept a well-stocked tool box. She rewired broken lamps. She glued back pieces of veneer that the antique furniture shed. She touched up the oil portraits of her ancestors, Caleb and Priscilla, with magic markers and black ball-point pens. She was always fixing the broken remnants of what she had inherited.

But my mother, when she was little Bobby, hated the dolls her mother Sadie gave her, although she never let on and kept the secret of her distaste to herself. The collection of antique dolls with china heads and bisque heads and hand-sewn gowns continued to grow as well intentioned friends of the family bestowed more dolls upon her for Christmas and birthdays. Eventually there was an article in The Daily Banner about her celebrated collection, with a photograph of my unsmiling mother surrounded by a mob of overdressed dolls.

Over and over in her life, Bobby was thwarted, prevented from doing what she might have done. In high school, she excelled at courses in the academic track and wanted to go to college at William and Mary. She boasted that she had the highest score on a standardized test for high-school students in the state of Maryland. She had inherited enough money to pay for her own higher education. But her mother forced her to go to National Park College, a two-year school for wealthy young ladies that her sister Sarah had attended in Washington, D.C. "Sadie made me go to a finishing school," Bobby said, "and it sure finished me."

She didn't get beyond her freshman year at National Park before events forced her to return home to take care of her mother, who was severely injured in the automobile accident that killed her sister Elizabeth, saved by the suitcase she held on her lap in the back seat. Accidents determined much of Bobby's life. She had to react to things that happened to her—deaths of loved ones and the birth of an only child, unexpected arrivals and sudden departures—and learn to be crafty and contrary, to act rashly and impulsively, to misbehave.

Paula Deitz and Ronald Koury
The Hudson Review
33 West 67th Street
New York, NY 10023

Dear Paula and Ron,

I'm sending you a xerox copy of my new book of translations — information that sestinas the chapters throughout the memoir. Aubrey's Lemon Grove includes two pieces on Aubrey, which come at the beginning but then I've placed in "backmatter" that separate the chapters. A few do not have personal information that essays and novels don't need. I have added personal information from the chapters that would be added in. Robin and I have revised the memoir — information that essays and novels don't need.

Best wishes,

August 26, 2014

Kenyon HH Avenue
Cincinnati, OH 15226
(513) 260-0571
aubrey@gmail.uc.edu

Why I Went to Summer Camp

Whenever I was bugging my mother in our apartment on Battery Lane, she liked to say, "Go outside and play in traffic." She didn't know what to do with me, probably because I was a boy and she was a single mother who had grown up with two older sisters. All I really wanted to do with the vast expanse of free time was to laze around the apartment, but my mother considered me hyperactive. She told me that Sadie, my grandmother, used to say, "Heavens, Bobby, that boy must have St. Vitus' dance! He just can't keep still." She wanted to channel that free time I was enjoying into something organized and supervised.

She found my first summer camp through a customer at the Wildwood branch of the Bank of Bethesda. It was located in northern Virginia, not far from Natural Bridge. The director called it Camp Fox Paw, and it was barely habitable. A handful of boys slept in a cabin with bunk beds, listening to twangy country-and-western songs on the counselor's radio, passing around *Mad* magazines and comic books. The only other building was a big structure on a hilltop, while the boys' cabin was down in a wooded holler. Girls, along with the director and his wife, stayed in what they called the lodge, which included the kitchen, dining hall, and activity room.

The camp had no structure and no schedule. It was spontaneous, absolute anarchy, and I loved it. Each morning at breakfast, we talked about what everyone wanted to do. One day we visited an antebellum mansion near the camp. One day we visited Natural Bridge. One day we went swimming in a pond with mud and weeds underfoot and leeches sucking our skin.

But some days we just hung around the lodge, everyone pursuing their own interests. One afternoon I spent hours swatting flies in the dining area, keeping a running count of my kills, like a flying ace from the First World War, and sneaking apples from the kitchen whenever I could. Another day I got scraps of wood, a hammer and some nails, and made what I called a cigarette machine. Another day a few of us ventured into the woods, looking for copperheads, thrilled by the prospect of danger.

I went to summer camp so my mother could have a respite from being a mother and could simply be Bobby, free to go on vacation with Carolyn. They drove to Cape Cod and stopped at Hyannis Port. At the gate of the Kennedy compound they tried to see if they could talk their way inside. They bragged about Carolyn's singing career: "She was the Gershwin girl. Rose and Ira Gershwin personally selected her for the tour. She sang for the Metropolitan Opera with Ezio Pinza. She gave concerts with Mario Lanza.

She made a recording with Eugene Ormandy." It was all true, if occasionally exaggerated. She didn't actually perform on the stage of the Met in New York, for example, but did sing many roles in the touring company's summer series at the Cincinnati Zoo.

The sweet-talking didn't work in Hyannis Port, where Secret Service agents, frowning under their sunglasses, waved them to turn around and get back on the highway. Bobby and Carolyn drove along the cape to Provincetown. What Bobby remembered most vividly about the trip was going into a big circus tent to watch movies. She and Carolyn saw *I Am Curious (Yellow)*, notorious then for its graphic sexuality (it came from Sweden, where mores were supposedly freer) but remarkably tame and even boring now.

For three years, I went to Camp Letts, which was located on a peninsula near the Chesapeake Bay—not for entire summer vacations but for two weeks to a month, enough time to correspond to my mother's vacations from the bank. It was a YMCA camp, so we had several religious services each week, outdoors in a clearing with pews made of fallen logs, a tree stump for the altar, and a cross made from straight branches tied together with rope. The camp didn't have a pool, so we swam in a netted area and had to watch out for jellyfish that slipped through the nets. The camp was not coeducational, so I missed having girls around. There were no horses, but there were plenty of boats, from canoes and rowboats to a schooner. Unfortunately, the camp was highly regimented, with reveille, assembly, and taps played by a bugle that blared from loudspeakers. Instead of the freedom we had enjoyed at Camp Fox Paw, we had to follow a strict schedule of activities. We had daily inspections, in which we lined up naked in our cabin and Doc Marino looked us over for ticks and, if he found none, slapped our rumps and said, "Next customer!" Back in school, I discovered that he wasn't a doctor at all but a substitute teacher. We also spent a lot of time at Camp Letts in custodial maintenance, cleaning our cabin, which looked like a barracks from World War II, scrubbing the latrine, and serving food and cleaning dishes in the dining hall, where flags from many nations hung from the rafters.

Before my second summer at Camp Letts, I spent a few days in Cambridge. I was playing badminton in the back yard with my cousin Dail, my cousin Ned, and my grade-school "girlfriend" who wore her hair in a ponytail. When I went to retrieve the shuttlecock that had flown into a garden plot near the back fence, I tripped over a wicket and braced the fall with my left wrist, which snapped. It looked like a fork viewed from the side, the bone not lining up. The girls ran into the house, crying. At the emergency room, Dr. Burdette forced the bone back into place with a quick, sickening crunch. Back at the house, I assured Cousin Audrey, with whom I was staying, that I knew how to break the news to my mother.

"Hi, Mom. Guess what?" I said on the phone. "I broke my arm!"

Audrey yanked the receiver from my right hand and said, "Now Bobby, don't you worry. It's not as bad as it sounds."

With my broken arm in a cast, I spent two weeks at Camp Letts, where I managed to play baseball, learning how to swing at pitches with one hand. But my mother always embellished the story and told people "He used his cast as a bat!"

My third year at Camp Letts was the worst, even though (or maybe because) I already knew some of the campers from home. Jimmy and Chuck were there from Battery Lane in Bethesda. My cousin Ned was there from Cambridge. They were all model campers, but I was such a slob and malcontent that I managed to get in trouble with a counselor named Tom. He kept track of etiquette violations, such as spilling bug juice on the tablecloth. He gave me several demerits when I refused to finish my oatmeal, after mixing in sugar, jam, and syrup in the hope that they would make it more palatable. In the evening, he exacted punishment in front of the assembled campers in our cabin. He might give the miscreant a swift kick, or sting him with a switch on the back of his legs, or use a boat oar to whack him on the butt. My mother became involved one day after Tom got mad at how messy I kept my upper bunk and open footlocker. He picked up my knapsack and snapped it at my head, opening a gash in the scalp with one of the buckles. Doc Marino tended to my wound in the infirmary. Bobby happened to be home when she got the call, so she drove to the camp immediately and confronted Tom, calling him a sadist, an abuser of the boys he was sworn to protect, a bad Christian, and someone who would lose his job on the spot and not get a reference for future employment if *she* had anything to say about it. He was sheepish, apologetic, and never bothered me after that.

I was lucky that the incident happened after Bobby had returned from two weeks at Lake Placid with Carolyn. They were used to living by the sea, since both had grown up in Tidewater Maryland, but the mountains were a novelty, so they liked to drive to resorts in the Adirondacks. They rowed on the lakes, got lost on the winding roads, hunted for antiques, and cuddled under the comforters on iron beds. Whatever else they did remained their secret. Freedom was the point. They still had to say they were cousins, in order to rent a room together, but otherwise their vacations could be as sweet as honeymoons.

Sometimes they drove to the Piedmont region of Western Maryland and stayed in a cottage at the Cozy Motel. They tried to get into the grounds of Camp David in the Catoctin Forest, but more Secret Service agents turned them away. In search of antiques, they drove up a dirt road and knocked on the door of a tarpaper shack. Inside, they realized their mistake when they looked around at the surprising number of silent, sullen, dirty, bearded men and frowsy women on couches, chairs, and chair arms. "We're looking for antiques, collectibles," Carolyn said. "Do you have any you'd be interested in selling?"

"No, ma'am," one of them said, but both Bobby and Carolyn were sure they expected some cash, like the keepers of a tollgate on a turnpike, before they'd let them leave. They ended up buying an old electric coffee pot with a frayed, wooly cord. Back in the car, Bobby said, "Those ridge runners really took us, didn't they, Carrie?"

"Just be grateful to Jehovah that we left that hovel in one piece. I've never been so scared in all my life." My mother put the coffee pot in the trash room when they returned home to Bethesda.

Disclosure #10

Sometimes, when Bobby was drinking and felt giddy instead of anguished, she talked about their "X-rated Polaroids." She told me, "You'd need asbestos gloves to handle them!" When I finally found them in a box in the linen closet, they were shots of Bobby and Carolyn sitting on the toilet, completely naked except for the panties around their ankles, squeezing their legs together to hide their privates, using their hands to cover their breasts, laughing uproariously. They looked so coy and flirtatious. That's what they did while I was at camp.

My mother became more and more comfortable about revealing her secrets to me, her only son, her confidant, the witness to her life, the secretary who took notes. "I was a virgin when I met your father," she told me, "and still a virgin when we got back from our honeymoon in Maine." They stayed at the Christmas Tree Inn, a sprawling red building that overlooked Highland Lake near Bridgton, Maine, and she informed my father that she was having her period, which wasn't true. He begged her, pleaded with her, since he was "hell-bent on getting married and having sex," but she wouldn't relent. That's not how she was brought up. That's not how a lady behaved. It wasn't hygienic. He'd just have to wait. She emphasized that she loved him, of course, but they couldn't have any marital relations while she was menstruating. He believed the lie for the rest of his life. When he was 87 years old, he confided to me that my mother was having her period during their honeymoon. "It's a miracle you were ever born," my mother once told me. "It took us six years. But at least you were planned."

Domestic Arrangements

Nothing much happened in the apartment my mother and I shared. She was worried about peeping Toms looking into the ground-floor bathroom by the driveway, so she painted a picture on the casement window: a sailboat on dark blue water under a pale blue sky. After I discovered the dirty books she kept in one of her antique dressers, she confronted me about it, since she was a clever detective. We carried on with our daily, undramatic lives.

One winter, after a heavy snowfall, I wanted to do her a favor, so I used a plastic scraper to remove snow from our Rambler American station wagon, but I didn't stop with the windshield and windows. I also scraped snow off the hood. When my mother told people about it—and she relished doing that for the rest of her life—she asserted that I'd scratched the paint job to hell with the jagged lid of an old tin can.

The most dramatic moment in that apartment happened when my mother told me that she and my father were getting divorced. "Now's the time," he wrote in a letter she showed me, "for me to ask you for my freedom." They had been separated for almost three years, and I was happy that my mother's closest partner was now Carolyn, but I still worried about the finality of the break between my parents. One afternoon, I barged into the bathroom where my mother had painted the sailboat on the window. She was unrolling her curlers and dropping them into a pink plastic bowl.

"Couldn't we move to New York?" I asked.

"He doesn't want us, the son of a bitch."

"Couldn't you both keep trying? See if something could be worked out?"

"Johnny, he doesn't want to patch things up. Forget it. It's water under the bridge now. I certainly don't want to set foot in New York City ever again. It breaks my heart, son, but he's such a jackass."

Soon after the divorce was final, my mother told me that my father was going to marry a woman named Cornelia. "She's in her forties, at least five years older than he is, and he just *had* to inform me," she paused to snicker, "that she's still a virgin."

When I arrived at their apartment on East 76th Street, Cornelia shook my hand with both of hers and said, "I'm *so* glad to *meet* you at last!" Then she extended an awkward hug. She had reddish hair, teased up a bit because it was thin, wore glasses, and had a pinched expression on her face. She was wearing a red plaid skirt, some kind of tartan, that exposed her knees. I was happier to make the acquaintance of Beau, her affectionate silver poodle.

My mother was gleeful when I reported back that Cornelia was not very good looking. "She sounds so prim and proper," my mother said, "like a real pill." She aided and abetted the instant resentment I felt for Cornelia. Nothing angered me more than when people I met in New York referred to her as my "mother." *My mother lives in Maryland,* I wanted to insist, although I always kept it to myself.

Cornelia's apartment was decorated with poodle figurines. They sat on bookshelves and tables and window sills. But the focal point of the apartment's one big L-shaped room was a Steinway grand piano by the big window. The top was down, covered by a tablecloth with fringe, as well as framed photographs, more poodle figurines, and a poinsettia in a pot, a gift from Van Cliburn and his mother. Cornelia knew the pianist because he was an RCA Victor recording artist whose producer was her boss. She also had an actual Grammy award, presented to the RCA engineers in 1959 for their recording of *The Marriage of Figaro*. They must have had a surplus, so they gave her a statuette and she placed it next to one of her many figurines of Nipper, the RCA Victor dog who listened to "his master's voice." He was positioned so one of his ears was cocked toward the bell of the brass gramophone.

"It couldn't be sex," my mother said when I showed her photographs of my trip to New York, "because she has no sex appeal." But my father and Cornelia were lovey-dovey enough, calling each other "Sweetie," saying everything was "lovely," playing a classical music radio station on their stereo. They had a wall of classical record albums, most of them from RCA Victor. They had a subscription to the Metropolitan Opera and took me to my first opera, *Aida*, at the old Met. When we went backstage afterwards, I met Leontyne Price, an RCA artist who had the limpest hand I ever shook. Carolyn Long had known her at Tanglewood, where they both had scholarships. "Yes, indeed," she told me when I returned home, "Leontyne and I were pals. She came from the deep south."

When Cornelia was nine, her parents brought her to New York so she could pick out her own Steinway grand piano, a seven-foot model B, at the showroom on 57th Street. "She wouldn't have anything else," my father said. "It had to be a Steinway." But I never heard her play a note. My father might sit down at the piano before dinner, while Cornelia was serving appetizers and drinks (Seven-Up with a twist for me and Whiskey Sours for them), and randomly play chords in some kind of atonal free-association, but she could not be cajoled into playing anything on her own piano. "Her teacher discouraged her from playing by ear," my father explained, "so she didn't know how to improvise. She had to have the music in front of her." Their world revolved around music, but none of it remained in her fingertips.

Even though they lived apart, Carolyn and Bobby still sought refuge together. Sometime during the early Sixties, they bought a ramshackle bungalow in North Beach, waterfront property on the western shore of the Chesapeake Bay, as a vacation retreat. My mother paid $8,000, as she did for every house she ever owned. It had a screen porch in the back, where we ate our meals at a picnic table, and a screen porch in front, where we rocked and enjoyed the breezes off the bay. It came entirely furnished, including the plates and silverware. There were three small bedrooms, each containing multiple beds, all lumpy, all provided with wrought-iron headboards. Our cats, Luigi and Ambrose, liked to race and skid down the linoleum of the long hallway. We couldn't swim in the bay because of the jellyfish, and we didn't own a boat—although both my mother and Carolyn knew how to sail—but we fished and spent a lot of time on the long, rickety pier, gazing across the bay and taking in the weather. There was a hammock strung between two of the shade trees in the big yard between the house and the bulwark the Army Corps of Engineers had built. We visited often and usually had guests in residence, my friends and theirs. But the neighboring houses were very close—you could touch the walls if you stood between them and stretched out your arms—and my mother became enraged when the family on one side built an L-shaped pier that interfered with our "water rights," turning at the end to encroach on the bay in front of our property. At least that was her excuse for getting rid of the bay house, selling it for $8,000, making no profit whatsoever. It's worth over sixty times that now, and it's frustrating that the paradise that belonged to us appreciated to the point that it was out of reach.

Although the bay place hadn't worked out, Bobby and Carolyn had enjoyed the taste of sharing a home and decided to pool their resources and move back in together. In November of 1963, we walked through a beautiful two-story house with a finished basement on Massachusetts Avenue. My mother promised that I could have a dog, and the two "cousins" signed a five-year lease with an option to buy.

Our private joy and hopefulness were undercut by the public tragedy of the Kennedy assassination. Both apartments were in disarray, with packed boxes stacked in the living rooms, but the three of us gathered in Carolyn's dining room to watch the news and mourn. In the evening, my mother and I walked over to the Naval Medical Center and waited for the President's body to arrive. "It's history," she said, "so we're going."

It was dark, but the tall white butte of the hospital was lit up. It looked like a movie premiere, searchlights turning, a huge crowd gathering. We walked over the golf links in front of the hospital and jostled against the throng near the helicopter landing pad. I remember my mother using her pocketbook to push our way through the mass of mourning fellow citizens. White-helmeted Military Police held hands to form a barricade to restrain the surging crowd, faces catching flashes of light and then filling with darkness. Finally, a helicopter approached and settled down noisily on the huge red cross on a white circle, the storm of its propeller blades slowly petering out. We saw a gunmetal coffin, which looked silver to me, and witnessed an honor guard lifting it, and then we saw the first lady. "There she is, Johnny," my mother said, clutching my arm, "It's Jackie. It's really her. Can you see her?" She was pretty far away, but we both thought we saw her, still wearing the blood-spattered pink outfit and pink hat, accompanied by an entourage of Secret Service agents, military personnel, and reporters, a woman alone in a clutch of men. It was a good thing that my mother always kept a handkerchief in her pocketbook, for she dabbed her eyes with it while she cried. Wind carried the odor of burning leaves.

We thought they had all descended in the helicopter, but in fact only the honor guard had flown. Jackie had taken a Navy ambulance, accompanying her husband's body from Andrews Air Force Base. It was a moment my mother wanted us both to remember, but inevitably our view was partial, obstructed, filled in by what we knew and imagined, as well as by what we observed. The thing that strikes me now as most remarkable is that my mother was willing and able to walk the considerable distance despite her bad knees. Navy Medical was close enough that we could hear a bugler play Taps after dark, and the tower was visible from the chain-link fence near our apartment building. But the grounds had to be at least half a mile from our building, and once we left the sidewalk along Rockville Pike, we had to make our way over the fairways and rough of the nine-hole golf course. And then we had to walk back. It may have been the farthest she ever walked as an adult, and she did it because of grief and because of our closeness to a historic moment. We had to go, no matter what.

Back at Carolyn's apartment, I searched through a stack of Washington *Posts,* ripping out one of the comic strips, "Miss Caroline," about a little girl living in the White House, crumpling them and shoving them into a grocery bag for the incinerator. I also threw out our copy of Vaughn Meader's comedy album, *The First Family,* which no longer struck me as funny. It was clear, however, that we were a family, the three of us, even if we were living in separate apartments. Tragedy had brought us together, that day, and moving to the house on Massachusetts Avenue would confirm the bond we shared. We hugged each other for consolation and spent the night there, me on the fold-out sofa in the room that once again served as a voice studio, now that the German boarders were gone, the two women in Carolyn's bedroom.

Disclosure #11

It was in the Glenwood apartment, when Carolyn was living across Battery Lane and my parents' divorce had become final, that my mother began to confide in me regularly, recounting the stories and some of the secrets of her life. She told me how she met my father on an overnight train, the Havana Special, coming up the Atlantic coast from Florida, where she had been visiting a friend in Tampa, a therapeutic vacation meant to help her recover from the shock of her sister's death in an automobile accident. "I had the upper berth of the sleeping car," she said, "because it was cheaper and Sadie was chintzy, even though it was my own money that Daddy left me in his will. Your father had the lower berth." He was a first lieutenant in the army, returning from Camp Davis, an antiaircraft artillery training center in North Carolina, where he had just completed an advanced course in radio-controlled airplanes. "He was a gentleman, so he helped me up the ladder. Nothing fresh, nothing forward." They exchanged addresses before she retired behind the curtain. When he woke up the next morning, she was already gone, having deboarded the train at Union Station in Washington. "He was so handsome in his uniform," my mother gushed, "He looked just like Gregory Peck. The first time I saw him in civilian clothes, I was so disappointed. 'You look like a jerk,' I said. He sulked around for the rest of the day."

World War II intensified brief encounters and stirred them up into romances. They exchanged a few letters and arranged a few dates, whenever he could get a weekend pass from Bethany Beach. She delighted in calling him a "ninety-day wonder" because he had become an officer through an accelerated program. On the beach in Delaware, he used a controller to guide a quarter-sized plane that was launched by a catapult. He christened it the Carolyn D, his bride's name painted on the tail fin, and could maneuver it as high as 10,000 feet, invisible to the naked eye, following its progress through a range finder. The 90-millimeter guns tracked it but didn't waste ammunition. They had target practice for that, firing at wind socks that were towed by planes above the ocean. When the Carolyn D ran out of gasoline and crashed in the Atlantic, my father rode out in a dinghy, equipped with an outboard motor, in search of the wreckage. Back on the beach, his men reassembled the pieces on a blanket so they could launch her again and track her flight. My mother kept photographs of him crouching beside the plane.

My grandmother Sadie approved of him because he knew the correct way to use a soup spoon, not toward himself but away, the direction less likely to risk spilling drops on a tablecloth. It goes to show that good manners may make us feel more comfortable but don't prove anything about the prospects for marital longevity.

Night Rumblings on Massachusetts Avenue

The house we moved into was two stories tall, the bricks painted white, although peeling paint let the red show through. The rent was high enough that my mother and Carolyn considered it risky to take up residence in such a fancy place. I had to change schools in the middle of eighth grade and leave my friends on Battery Lane, but one of the inducements was that my mother promised I could get a dog. I reminded her about the promise, once we were living there, but she said, "Aren't the cats enough? You wouldn't walk it anyway. I'd be the one who had to do it." She was right, of course.

In many ways, we were elated to live there. We spent a lot of time at the picnic table on the patio, which felt secluded because it was surrounded on three sides by the back of the house, the detached garage, and a solid row of arborvitaes. The open side looked out on an apple tree. There was also, at the back end of the property, a cherry tree that actually produced cherries. That yard provided the only place my mother ever spent much time gardening. She claimed that she accidentally mixed up some seeds and produced a hybrid that was half zinnia, half tomato. "When you cut them open," she said, "they looked like zinnias inside. We sliced them into salads. Carolyn said they were already seasoned."

Originally, they slept in the two front bedrooms and I slept in the addition at the rear of the second floor. Carolyn used the living room as her voice studio, after deciding that the knotty-pine basement was too cold and damp.

When I went to the kitchen for a snack after school, someone would inevitably be running through scales or launching into a song, which Carolyn interrupted again and again. She kept a big, round, magnifying mirror on top of the upright so the student could see what his or her mouth was doing during the song. Ambrose, the Siamese cat, liked to sit on top of the piano and look down the singers' throats as they performed. The worse the singer, the more she seemed to enjoy their warbling, especially an older woman who had a wobble in her voice.

I had a big crush on a teenage pupil named Kristin who had long, dark, wavy hair and wore braces. After I got out of the army, about seven years later, she had resumed taking voice lessons with Carolyn, and the two of us went on a date that took us to Georgetown and then to the National Cathedral. Her hair was cut short, and at one point she gamboled ahead of me in a frisky way before we entered the cathedral. It looked like flirting, and I'm surprised that I never asked her out again.

Some of Carolyn's students were memorable for better reasons. Naomi Weaver brought her own accompanist to the house, a student at Howard

University named Roberta Flack. After the pianist became a pop singer with hits such as "The First Time Ever I Saw Your Face" and "Killing Me Softly," my mother delighted in bragging that she had come to our house, even though I don't believe she ever sang a note there.

Carolyn met another one of her students when someone, possibly Naomi, recommended that we come to an inner-city gospel service and listen to the tenor there. His name was Willie Brown, and Carolyn was so impressed that she offered to give him lessons for free, which he accepted. I remember how commandingly he sang Handel's "Sound an Alarm," and I even sent a snippet from the reel-to-reel tape of his lesson to a friend in California as part of a sound collage. Carolyn gave him an introduction to her friend Morton Gould, but somehow he became suspicious of her intentions, stopped taking voice lessons with her, and struck out on his own, formalizing his professional name, as she had suggested, to William Brown, and went on to have a nice career of his own. Carolyn always believed, however, that he could have gone much farther if he had used her connections instead of turning on her.

One of Carolyn's former accompanists, Stan Carter, stayed with us several times. Once, at our kitchen table, I was sitting with Stan and the boyfriend he brought along for the visit. "You have such a beautiful face," Stan told me. "Doesn't he, Johnny? Doesn't he have a beautiful face? Classic look, strong jaw-line. You really should be in modeling." Maybe my acne was in remission then, but usually my face was spotted with pimples and minuscule puncture marks where I had popped them. Nothing solved the problem, not Stridex pads, not Clearasil lotion painted over the tiny volcanic mounds, not giving up chocolate ice cream and potato chips, not sunning my face as I lounged on the patio. The remedy that finally cleared up my complexion, wiping away the blemishes almost instantly, was a prescription for birth-control pills.

We had multiple doctors, probably because of differences in how receptive they were to honoring prescription requests, but our main physician at the time was gruff old Dr. Ryland, whom Carolyn considered "a superb diagnostician." During a routine check-up, he observed several red streaks across my back. "What are you two doing to that boy?" he demanded. "Am I going to have to report you to the authorities?" I guessed that the welts may have been caused by my leaning back in class, when the edge of a chair's back pressed sharply against my ribs. Carolyn believed that the older brother of one of my friends, who used to crack a bullwhip in the parking lot of the Glen Aldon Apartments, had flogged me. But they were probably stretch marks from a growth spurt.

Carolyn saw herself as a psychic. I remember asking, when some sort of news bulletin interrupted a game show we were watching, "Did you know that was going to happen?"

"I did," she said. "This must be one of my periods of clairvoyance. I'm a sympathetic soul. I'm picking up things from all over right now."

She wasn't enough of a psychic, however, to realize what a mistake it was to pay for a first-class ticket on an ocean liner so Anita, her maid when she was living in Milano and studying at La Scala, could travel to America and live in our house. Anita was nasty to everyone but Carolyn, didn't want to be a cleaning lady in America, refused to learn a word of English, and took over the den on the first floor. All of us had been happy she was coming, but she ruined that goodwill immediately. I was hoping to learn some Italian, but she sneered at me, so I gave up. My mother did learn some, probably because she tried harder and was the one in charge of running the household. Carolyn spoke Italian fluently, but she too became disenchanted. Anita wasn't the same. She stayed with us a year, and the only thing I remember is how part of the house, the den where she was holing up, was off-limits. When my mother and Carolyn ordered her to leave, they still had to pay for her trip back to Italy, but this time she traveled third-class on the last voyage of the Cristoforo Colombo, in the bottom of the ship, where she roomed with three or four other people.

Although Anita had proven herself a faithless retainer, we were luckier in our other guests. Carolyn got back in touch with Ruth Small, a classmate from the Peabody Conservatory, who frequently brought her family to the house and welcomed us to theirs, also located on Massachusetts Avenue but very close to the National Cathedral, much larger and more prominent than the over-priced place we rented.

Ruth's teenage son, Hal, had long curly hair—the whole family had sleepy looking eyes—and played organ in a rock band called The Lunatic Fringe. One evening, during a practice session, I embarrassed myself in the huge living room of their house when I screamed and squealed my way through "Satisfaction" like a pipsqueak imitator of Mick Jagger. For the rest of their lives, whenever they saw me, Ruth and her husband Haskell mentioned that performance, complimenting not my voice but my bravery.

Ruth and Colonel Small looked as though they had just come from the mad tea party in *Alice in Wonderland*: nervous, hesitant, flustered, but also good-spirited. They didn't look rich, and their house didn't look like the residence of millionaires, nothing like the ostentatious mansion my mother had forsaken when she rejected creepy Uncle Guy's marriage proposal. But the Smalls were accomplished, cultivated, artistic, intellectual, and generous with their money, patrons of the arts in Washington. Unlike Carolyn, Ruth had earned her degree at Peabody.

Life in the daytime was good in our house on Massachusetts Avenue. We had never lived in such luxury, with wall-to-wall carpeting, a screen porch, a working fireplace, our first dishwasher, laundry facilities in the basement, multiple bathrooms, a formal dining room, and more bedrooms than we needed. I had a paper route, and on Sunday mornings Carolyn and my mother told me to load the stacks of Washington *Posts* into the car so they could help me deliver them. They grumbled about it, but it was a bond we shared instead of going to church.

At night, though, everything was different, once they had started drinking. It was a ritual, so the outcome varied only by degrees. Fireworks typically began after dinner, perhaps because Carolyn was a stickler for good table manners. She always ordered me not to saw with my knife when I cut into a steak, but I couldn't get the knack of separating the meat properly.

The fights began as eruptions of noise, their voices rising in volume, Carolyn's low and droning, my mother's high as a shriek. They went back and forth from bedroom to bedroom, giving each other hell and slamming the doors as they left. It was impossible to ignore the skirmishing when I was on the same floor, so at some point I had to emerge from my room and intervene. I thought of myself as a diplomat, a go-between who negotiated peace agreements between hostile factions. I reminded myself that Massachusetts Avenue was also known as Embassy Row. It amused me—in a wry, not entirely joyous way—to think of myself as part of the corps that had diplomatic immunity, even though the ambassadors and attachés were all stationed miles away, on the other side of the district line.

It wasn't long before I moved downstairs to the recreation room in the basement. Even two floors below, however, I wasn't shielded from their fights. My paneled room felt like a bunker, a bomb shelter where the explosions at night became more terrifying because I couldn't see what was happening.

And they conducted many of their pitched battles in the kitchen. Carolyn once held a paring knife to my mother's throat while they sat at the table all night long, although that sounds like one of my mother's exaggerations. They became distrustful of each other. My mother watered down the vodka, but Carolyn responded by drawing a pencil line on the bottle after she poured herself a drink so she could see if the level of pure liquor had been compromised.

There was too much conflict, too much nightly commotion, for things to go on like that, so we didn't last beyond the halfway point of our five-year lease. The darkness outweighed the considerable light. And we all felt like failures.

Disclosure #12

I often had friends staying at the house for sleepovers, and they tried to steer clear of Carolyn, who must have intimidated them. But there may have been another reason why one of them avoided her. Once, when she was drunk, she summoned us to her bedroom and held out the big, white, plastic goose she had named Radames, after the tenor in Aida, although she always called him "Rotten Eggs." She commanded, with some solemnity, "Kiss My Goose!" We all suppressed our laughter, backed out of the room, and bounded downstairs from the second floor to the basement. Carolyn claimed that later that night, one of the boys, who would have been 15 or 16, snuck into her room and tried to get in bed with her, asking her to take off her clothes and let him touch her breasts, which were prodigious. My friend always denied her accusation, but he made sure he avoided her.

Breaking Up and Getting Back Together

Whenever someone at one of our picnics dropped a hot dog or a burger on the ground, my mother was quick to pick it up, wipe it off, and put it back on the plate or the bun, always saying, "You've got to eat a peck of dirt before you die." I knew the word *peck* from a song she sang when I was little, "I love you... a bushel and a peck... a bushel and a peck and a hug around the neck," and I figured it was bigger than a bushel basket, but I wasn't sure how much dirt could fit in a container of that size. I didn't realize until years later that the saying was figurative and meant you had to eat a lot of shit in a lifetime.

My mother was sick of putting up with Carolyn, worn out by their drunken fights, so she rented a two-bedroom apartment in a garden-apartment complex, back on Battery Lane, and the two of us moved out. Carolyn rented a studio apartment in a huge, impersonal building called the Greenbriar that was also on Massachusetts Avenue but in the District of Columbia, not Maryland. She didn't like reminiscing about her time there because the separation was hellish for her. Only one story survived—hardly even a story, just a weekly ritual. On Sundays, Carolyn put Ambrose, the Siamese cat that was staying with her, in a grocery cart and took her across the street through the woods to an abandoned colonial mansion on the grounds of American University, where Carolyn worked as an adjunct instructor of voice.

On Battery Lane, my mother couldn't bother me about mowing the lawn or shoveling snow, since we no longer had a yard. Things were calmer, but there was still plenty of tension between us, mainly because I was moody and had fallen into the clutches of rock and roll. I wanted to join a band, write songs, and go to concerts, motivated by the notion that it would help me attract girls. I had the same incentive for getting involved with a born-again Christian youth group that met for breakfast once a week in the basement of a Presbyterian church where Carolyn had once sung, not realizing that those girls were not the ideal targets for my erotic wishful thinking. The outward and visible sign of my inward and spiritual rebellion was letting my hair grow longer.

"You look like Ish Kabibble!" my mother taunted, although I had no idea who that might be. When I finally saw a picture of the comedian, I was insulted. He had a bowl-cut like Moe Howard of the Three Stooges but looked much homelier. I hated what I called her nagging, and my response was to ignore her. One of Carolyn's pet names for my mother was Haglet Metalhead, which I altered to Naglet Meddlehead.

She threatened to kick me out of the apartment if I didn't march myself to Elmer's Barber Shop and get a haircut. I had bangs, my attempt at imitating the early Beatles haircut, but I was a couple of years too late, since by that time the trendsetters wore their hair below their shoulders, like Jesus Christ. "I'm ashamed to be seen with you," my mother complained. "If you don't get a haircut, you'll have to move to New York and live with your father."

It's unlikely that he or Cornelia would have agreed to this new arrangement, which my mother probably considered cruel and unusual punishment for everyone involved. Their life was never tumultuous, except when I visited and acted surly, or when my mother phoned because she was irked or enraged by how my father was not providing enough support. Their life was comfortable and complacent. Both my father and stepmother kept date books and recorded what happened in their daily lives: operas they attended, trips they made, friends and relatives who had visited them, what they ate for dinner at restaurants. They kept records of regularity, testaments of contentment. They made sure they got their drama in the opera house, not at home.

Despite my posturing, I was a good boy who did not want to leave home, so I went to Elmer's Barber Shop and asked him not to take off too much. He ignored my request and overdid the clipping, leaving no hair hanging over my ears. It turned out that the mother of one of my friends had goaded her about my long hair and recommended that she kick me out of the apartment if I didn't comply. "After you stormed out," she told me later, "I cried. I wasn't sure if you were going to get a haircut or leaving for good."

My mother's instinct, apart from the interference of her prim and proper friends, was to be generous and indulgent. Before I learned to drive, she served as my chauffeur when I went out on dates. When I got my license, she not only let me use the car to take out girls but allowed me to drive myself to school and had someone from the bank pick her up and take her to work. When I needed money, I opened my wallet so it looked like a mouth and said, "Feed me!"

It wasn't long before Carolyn moved to her own two-bedroom apartment across the parking lot. Diplomatic relations were reestablished. They couldn't stay apart forever, but now they knew that living together was perilous. We often had dinner at Carolyn's place, where she'd try out new recipes on us. The two of them went out on what I would now consider dates. When they were having cocktails in the Silver Fox, Carolyn started playing the piano, but the management stopped her when they discovered she didn't have a union card.

Their most public outing as a couple happened when they attended my high-school graduation together. My father and Cornelia sat elsewhere, farther back in the geodesic dome that served as the gymnasium and auditorium of Walt Whitman High School. Carolyn didn't approve of how I slouched across the stage when I got my diploma, telling me, "Johnny, you need to improve your posture. Stand up straight as a ramrod, not stoop-shouldered!" But she and my mother were both teary-eyed and radiant, my number one set of parents, proud of their boy.

Disclosure #13

I visited my father and Cornelia at least twice a year when I was growing up, and the culmination of every trip was the debriefing session when I told my gleeful mother about the stupid things they had said and the pointless things we had done. My father always did his best to entertain me, taking me to something special like the World's Fair, or the Cloisters, or a baseball game, or the Circle Line boat ride around Manhattan, or a short-lived amusement park called Freedomland, but the most I could grant was that he was cordial, and that word didn't sound right for a parent's affection for his child.

Prodigal Son in the Army

During my second year at the University of Maryland, I shared a one-bedroom apartment with a fellow undergraduate from the trailer that had served as our dormitory when we were freshmen. One afternoon, during Christmas break when my roommate was away, my mother came over for a visit. While I sat in the living room, reading the newspaper she had brought as a gift or a distraction, she lingered in the bedroom and searched through the mess on my roommate's desk. When she emerged, she looked sheepish. "I have to apologize," she said. "When you snoop, you always find what you don't want to find. I was looking through your friend's papers, and I found an envelope, which was open, and God forgive me, I pulled the letter out and read it, which I shouldn't have. It was from some boy in the army—"

"You mean Lance?"

"—and he talked about how they had sex here when he was visiting, and how he hoped the first experience wasn't too upsetting, and how he'd found a lover in California, someone in his barracks."

"You mean at language school?"

"Yes, I suppose. Forgive your poor old mom?"

What interested me wasn't the account of homosexual relations in the bedroom I shared with my roommate but the reminder that the Armed Forces offered a language school in Monterey, California. What was loitering at the back of my mind, as I floundered in doubt about where my life was heading, jumped to the front. I wasn't maintaining enough credits at the university to keep my student deferment and was worried that my low number in the draft lottery might get me sent to fight in Vietnam. Without my mother's nosiness, her detective's knack for uncovering evidence, I might not have started thinking seriously about enlisting to learn German at the language school. But now the idea sounded like a possible way to make a fresh start—not to meet people or have titillating experiences, but to begin transforming myself. The good thing about the army would be that I'd have to keep on going, doing the assignments I was ordered to do, or be court-martialed, and that sounded like enough incentive to keep me studying.

In the middle of April 1970, I decided to enlist in the army, and my mother was the first person I told. She was worried, but she was also relieved that I wouldn't be drafted and sent off to war. She liked my plan to take time off from college and learn a foreign language. Still, it meant I'd be far away from her for three years, and that contributed to her ambivalence. "Whatever you do," she said, "you know I'll be proud of you." After that, she always told people that I joined the army to get discipline, but that was an oversimplification.

In basic training at Fort Dix, soon after we were issued our uniforms, they marched us into an office in the barracks to have our portraits taken. When the photographer's assistant, a young woman in uniform who was taking orders for picture assortments, asked for my home address, I wouldn't tell her, another pipsqueak refusal. She didn't press the issue but simply smiled and said it was okay. I didn't want any photographs of me in the short-sleeved khaki shirt, open at the collar to show a triangle of white tee-shirt and the chain holding my dog-tags, a hat tilted slightly on my shaved head, to surface or survive. I didn't want that visual record, that proof of my service in the army, to exist outside of a file cabinet. But the army got in touch with my mother anyway and said something like "Surely your son meant for you to know about this once-in-a-lifetime offer for something you will treasure forever." So she bought the maximum number of the photographs I detested, the evidence I wanted to destroy. Years later, whenever I visited the house of someone who knew my mother, there it would be, me in my uniform under the brim of the stiff hat, framed and propped on top of the television.

When I got a weekend pass, my mother reserved a room at the Bellevue Stratford Hotel in Philadelphia, and my father took a bus from Manhattan to join us for dinner at Bookbinder's Restaurant, where I ordered shrimp cocktail, filet mignon, and lobster tail. It was the first time since my parents' divorce, nine years earlier, that the three of us had been together. I ate too much for dinner, felt bloated, and went to bed early while they stayed up talking, probably worrying about their boy who was trying to get some discipline but having a hard time. My father left that night while I was asleep. On Sunday morning, room-service delivered breakfast, including blueberries and fresh-squeezed orange juice. My mother, relaxed and prolonging our time together, sipped coffee and pointed out the cornices and wainscoting of the old-fashioned room, telling me, "Those are the last vestiges of an elegant age."

A few days after the weekend in Philadelphia, I sprained my ankle during a training exercise. X-rays showed a hairline fracture, and the doctor put on a plaster cast and gave me crutches to use for hobbling around. I also received a medical profile that excused me from marching, going on bivouac, running the obstacle course, throwing hand grenades, and crawling under live machine-gun fire. Back home, after she heard the alarming news, my mother told her friends that I had broken thirteen little bones in my foot.

She always enjoyed exaggerating, but my struggles in the army inspired her to new heights of invention. Eventually, even though I never rose higher than Specialist Fifth Class, she started to address her letters to me as "Lieutenant." It's no coincidence that it was my father's rank when he was an antiaircraft officer during World War II. But I seethed with resentment that she felt it necessary to give me a promotion so she could impress her friends. I sent her money when I lived in Germany, but she inflated the numbers. It struck me that she was making excuses for me, embarrassed to admit the truth, believing that I should have contributed more.

On my last day at Fort Dix, after a ceremony on the parade ground, I waited for my mother and Carolyn to drive to New Jersey and pick me up outside the post library, where I was pacing on the wooden porch, my ankle much better now that I was done with basic training. Hours passed, and I started worrying that they had been involved in an accident, a crash on the turnpike, and might be injured or worse. When she finally got there, seven hours late, she was annoyed that I had made her drive all that way to pick me up when all I had was "one little bag," meaning my heavy duffel bag of uniforms. "Mom," I said, "I thought you might be dead! I was worried sick." She explained that they were late because the air conditioning in the rental car didn't work right so she went back to exchange the car for another model. She was irked, sweating and swearing, red-faced and fuming, and reminded me that she was not in the taxicab business, especially when I could have taken the bus or the train, but that didn't stop her from clutching me in a fierce hug and saying, "My boy's back!"

Years later, I boasted about how it was a miracle the army didn't recycle me and make me take basic training all over again and force me to lose my orders to language school to learn German, so I might have ended up in Advanced Infantry Training with orders for combat in Vietnam. My mother informed me that Louis Goldstein, the longtime Comptroller of the state of Maryland and one of Carolyn's old friends, had made some phone calls on my behalf, so I was waived through to language school at the Defense Language Institute in Monterey, California. My mother and Carolyn had saved me.

Another intervention helped get my orders changed from Military Police to Interrogation School when I was finishing the 32-week course in German. I had actually begged my mother, in a letter home, to write to our Congressman for help. And it took the two of them, working together to smooth the way for the boy they had raised together, Carolyn supplying the political connection, my mother giving a push.

They were my main sources of correspondence while I was in the army. Nowhere was I lonelier than in West Germany, posing as a civilian at a refugee camp in Zirndorf, a suburb of Nuremberg, serving as a low-level spy in Military Intelligence. While I was living by myself in the attic of a rooming house whose landlady told me she "hated Americans," they sent me care packages that always contained newspapers, literary magazines, and things to eat or drink: Bundt cakes still in the pans, bouillon cubes, tea bags, crackers, tins of cookies, cans of sardines, and plastic bags of Maryland beaten biscuits.

In the middle of October, during my last year in the army, I received a cryptic telegram from Carolyn: "John call us upstairs in the next 24 hours. Carrie Long." The post office was right next door to my house on Bahnhofstrasse, so I rushed there to make a phone call home. I was afraid that something terrible had happened to my mother or that some crisis had erupted. It turned out that Carolyn's ex-husband Blair, the Marine lieutenant colonel who had stormed Iwo Jima, sent her a check for $10,000 after Carolyn returned a silver tray and flatware that belonged to his family.

At first, my mother and Carolyn considered using the money to open a general store, which would have been a fiasco, but they decided, instead, to use part of the proceeds to help my mother take a trip to Europe so she could visit me and we could travel to Italy together. Carolyn gave her the money for her round-trip plane ticket, and I paid for our hotels and rented a Volkswagen. My mother was thrilled, but she was also sad that Carolyn wasn't well enough to accompany her.

We started in Nuremberg and then drove to Florence, Venice, Munich, and then back to Nuremberg. The low point of our trip took place on the drive to Florence, through tunnels, across viaducts, amid heavy traffic with lots of trucks, tinier than in America, our Volkswagen huge amid Fiats, everyone speeding, swerving, careening, weaving in and out around the sharp curves. All of a sudden, my mother exclaimed, "Oh, Johnny, look at that! A baby's coffin!"

I saw a long, plain, wooden box in back of one of the flatbed trucks. I thought it was probably something else, perhaps a crate of rifles, not a coffin. "It might be," I replied.

"No, look, it's the right size, just the right shape." Cars veered across our path. "It's so sad," she said, starting to weep, probably thinking of me as an infant and how unbearable the grief would have been. The mountains rose steeply around us, and down below were vineyards and a river.

"It might be. Could be. But how should I know? It's a box."

"No, it's a coffin for a little baby. Why do you always contradict me?" My mother's face was turning red, her cheeks wet with tears when I glanced over. "Listen," she said. "I've just about had enough."

Vehicles zigzagged on the curvy highway while I was pounding on the steering wheel, both of us furious, as usual, until I saw a hearse pull up beside us, loaded with a small mahogany coffin. "Oh, there it is!" I said.

We laughed at the misunderstanding, although my mother was quick to say, "Oh, no, we shouldn't be laughing. The little coffin is so pitiful, so sad." But things were back to normal between us, despite the death we accompanied on the crowded, twisting highway, for I was still her son and we were together, at least for two weeks, driving through the Apennines.

The high point took place in Venice, when we visited the lovely Church of the Miracoli. She didn't, in fact, want to go inside, so she waited outdoors, sitting and smoking by the bridge over the nearby canal. When I emerged, she was excited. She pointed to the side of the bridge, where someone had drawn a picture, a dark silhouette. "That's my little church," she said, just as she had claimed the Palazzo Dario as "my house" when we rode a *vaporetto* down the Grand Canal. The discovery mattered because it was hers, even though she had no particular interest in the vaulted, marble-veneered Renaissance church, often described as a "jewel box." The little sketch became her mental property, and she had me take a photograph of it. A couple of decades later, when I returned to the spot, the picture was gone. A new bridge had replaced the one where my mother had noticed something that pleased, delighted, and comforted her, something that became one of her treasures for the rest of her life.

Disclosure #14

Later in the 1970s, after I saw **One Sings, the Other Doesn't,** *a film directed by Agnès Varda, I found the title useful for explaining which Carolyn was which when I told people about my complicated family. But Carolyn Long, the opera singer, always called my mother by her nickname, Bobby. One day, when I was seven or eight, my mother said to me, "What do you know? We're cousins!" So they became Cousin Bobby and Cousin Carolyn, and it made things simpler—but not for me. Since I thought of cousins as kids my own age that I was related to, I started calling Carolyn Long my aunt, and friends and relatives either corrected me ("She's not your aunt!" "She's my cousin then." "She's not your cousin either!") or became noticeably silent when I happily, innocently, proudly referred to her.*

Keeping a Schedule

When I returned from Europe and the army, I spent a year living on Battery Lane in my mother's new one-bedroom apartment. It was located directly above Carolyn's studio, and commerce between the two residences was frequent. There might as well have been a staircase between the two floors, like the one that Marilyn Monroe opens up so she can drift down to Tom Ewell's flat in *The Seven-Year Itch*. As it was, we had to leave my mother's place, walk down a flight of stairs, exit the building, descend from the stoop, walk around a huge bush I once trimmed as part of a summer job my mother found for me, and walk down a few more steps to Carolyn's place, which consisted of two rooms and a bathroom. You entered into a space that served as living room, dining room, and kitchen. It had a fold-out sofa that Carolyn slept on—except that she never folded it out. There probably wasn't enough room, but years of scrunching up on lumpy cushions didn't help Carolyn's deteriorating spine. The kitchen was basic, just a corner with a sink, a stove, and a small refrigerator. My mother had refinished a low, long bookcase, painted it glossy black, and then covered the back and sides with contact paper that looked like red burlap. Carolyn used it as room divider, pantry, cupboard, and food preparation area. There wasn't enough space for a dining room table, so we ate dinner on TV trays.

The other room was bigger and must have been intended as a bedroom, but Carolyn used it as her voice studio. It contained her black Baldwin upright piano, her huge reel-to-reel Sony tape recorder, and her antique furniture. The framed pictures reflected her interests and tastes: the death mask of Beethoven that terrified me when I was a boy, two Japanese prints of geishas, an engraving of a classical scene by Poussin, and a colorful oil painting she had bought from one of her students, a gigantic scene of a big city, viewed over the water at sunrise or sunset, probably inspired by Manhattan, garish in red, yellow, and orange. It looked apocalyptic to me, like a city on fire, but I think she loved it for its drama and bright colors.

Often enough, I slept downstairs, where I could enjoy the privacy, and Carolyn joined my mother upstairs. Tippi Wong, the Siamese cat that Carolyn named after a restaurant owner in New York, might stay down or go up. But we often ate together downstairs in her studio apartment. Carolyn prided herself on her cooking, and her specialties included scallops marinated in sauterne and sautéed in butter, served with a blend of potatoes and parsnips.

Both of them smoked, and I hated the way that, at the end of a meal, they would crush their cigarettes by sticking them into the remains of the mashed potatoes and parsnips. Both of them drank, and that made me abstain, at least in their presence. I was still the designated diplomat who had to intervene when they started to quarrel.

The fights always happened at night, sometime after cocktail hour, but they didn't happen on most nights, at least not in my presence. When my mother got drunk, she turned manic, her face red, her voice pitched higher, everything about her accelerated like a sports car over the speed limit. When Carolyn got drunk, everything slowed down, her movements more deliberate, her soprano voice lower.

One night, after dinner, when both of them had drunk more than they'd eaten, my mother, whose face was bright red, said to me, "I think it's time I told you something about me and your father. It involves Carolyn too." She rolled the ice around in her tumbler and took a sip of her drink. "I think you're old enough to know. It happened when we were living in Cambridge. Your father started it, but all three of us were in on it. We kept a schedule."

She took another sip, and Carolyn looked over from the kitchen corner. My mother and I were sitting on the sofa. "Bobby, what are you saying?" Carolyn intoned.

"Johnny," my mother continued, "we kept a schedule of who was going to sleep with Carolyn, your father or me."

"Bobby!" Carolyn interrupted. "It isn't so."

"Oh yes it is, son. I'm not proud of it, but we took turns. We made a little calendar, whose night it was to spend with her. We shared Carolyn."

"How long did you do *that*, the three of you?" I asked.

"Not long," my mother said.

"Not at all," Carolyn said, "Not a word of what she's saying is true."

"Oh, yes it is, Carolyn, and you know it. You can deny it all you want, but it's true, true, true." My mother was sobbing. Carolyn, wearing a dramatic red robe, walked slowly past us into her voice studio and shut the door.

For all her bawdiness and risqué stories, Carolyn could be a prude, like many strip-tease artists who performed in burlesque theatres, and for all her good upbringing and manners, my mother could be lewd and indecent. Drinking brought out these apparent contradictions in both of them. I always thought that bourbon, my mother's "sody pops," which she mixed with Coca-Cola, acted like a truth serum. The more she drank, the redder her face turned and the more confessions flowed from her mouth, the id pouring through the sluice gate of a dam.

The next morning, over breakfast upstairs, with Carolyn still sleeping on her sofa down below, my mother apologized, telling me, "Son, I'm mortified that I acted like the Madwoman of Chaillot last night. Please forgive me—and forget what I said."

"But is it true?" I asked.

"Just forget it, please?"

Neither of us mentioned that night's revelation for over three decades. My mother must have forgotten she ever divulged it. But when she was confined to a nursing home because of her emphysema, several weeks before entering hospice care, after I had signed papers for the cremation she demanded because she was afraid of being buried alive like a doomed maiden in a tale by Edgar Allan Poe, my mother said, "I promised that one day I'd tell you all my secrets, son. Well, here's something you'll be interested in hearing, something for the book you're writing about me. Carolyn, your father, and I—back in Cambridge before the damned fool ran away to New York—the three of us kept a schedule."

"Oh, I know about that," I said.

"You do?"

"Yes, you told me about it one night when you were both drinking in Carolyn's basement studio."

"I must have been really tight. I don't remember a thing. Honest."

"You both were. You confessed that you made up a schedule for who got to sleep with Carolyn. She denied it, by the way."

"Yes, she would, wouldn't she?" my mother said, looking at the ceiling as she lay in her hospital bed. She had clear plastic cannulae, attached to an oxygen machine, up her nostrils. On the covers, one of her arthritic hands was rubbing the other. She tilted her head toward me and said, "Don't make the same mistakes I did, son. The sex doesn't last very long."

Disclosure #15

When my mother was a teenager, she enjoyed having a network of boyfriends, a circle of admirers who could take her to dances or the lover's lane she referred to as "Queer Action Hill," a name I found odd because there were so few hills in the marshy land of Dorchester County. When it snowed, we sledded down a pathetic little slope next to the court house, a grassy depression optimistically called Spring Valley. My guess is that she was alluding to Sandy Hill, a spot where we used to hunt unsuccessfully for arrowheads. Now the area is built up, but back then it would have been relatively secluded. Still, no one I've asked about Queer Action Hill has ever heard about it, and I've asked people my mother's age, including one of those boyfriends. The "queer action" sounds like a Freudian invention of my mother's.

She played off one boyfriend against another to make them jealous. She'd break up with Calvin and get back with Larry, or Leonard, or Phil (another Phil, not my father). She was afflicted with Southern Belle disease. Maybe it was over-compensation on her part, trying to stir up some enthusiasm about eligible young men. Maybe it was the genteel, flirtatious tradition she learned at home in her Victorian house, a minor-league version of Scarlett O'Hara's Tara, or at the finishing school she attended for a year, or through the Daughters of the American Revolution, of which she was a member until I badgered her into resigning because, even as a thirteen-year-old, I was passionate about the civil rights movement.

My mother was remarkably frank about her erotic life after my father abandoned us. She told me that what she really liked was necking—kissing and embracing—more than sex, at least with men. She must have been a horrible tease in high school, flirting with the boys, encouraging them, and then turning away, snubbing them. Switching from one boyfriend to another acted like an escape hatch she slipped through when things got too serious, too close to the real thing.

I remember when we were watching James Garner on television, in the 1970s, and my mother gushed, "He really makes my toes curl." It was one her stock phrases, whenever she saw a good-looking actor, and it irked me because it seemed like a disingenuous attempt to convince others, and perhaps herself, that her erotic interests were heterosexual. It was like see-through camouflage that couldn't hide her loving and living with (at least off and on) a woman instead of a man.

Her first boyfriend was Ralph. "When was that?" I asked.

"Oh, let's see," she said, "when I was about eight. He only lived in Cambridge for a few months. He came in the fourth grade. Good looking? Oh God, yes. I used to beg our neighbor Addie to take me to Washington so I could stay with her at the Y and visit Ralph and his mother. She was a proper Englishwoman. He used to take me out to dinner when we were living in Bethesda and he was passing through. I should have married Ralph."

And so it was with her gallery of boyfriends. She should have married each and every one of them, as she lamented. Ralph became a fighter pilot during World War II and was decorated for his aerial exploits. Among my mother's most precious stack of mementoes, kept in a tin box, was a group of newspaper clippings, some celebrating the "abnormally keen eyesight" that explained his prowess as a pilot, but some reporting his arrest on morals charges. He was convicted and "given a two-year suspended sentence" for "performing indecent acts in his bedroom window, in view of three small neighborhood children."

Leonard was going to marry my mother after the war was over. When he returned, on leave from the army, to visit his mother and sister in their apartment above the Arcade Theatre, he was wearing his uniform when my mother finally got up the nerve to see him. "I'm so sorry, Leonard," she said, "but I'm engaged. I meant to write you a letter, but I just couldn't sit myself down and start to explain and excuse my behavior."

"That's all right, darling," he said, "don't you worry about it." He wasn't hurt at all. Maybe he was even relieved.

Larry, who was a year younger, took her sailing on the river and escorted her to the senior prom. They had started dating when she was in ninth grade. "We were both unattached," Larry told me on a trip I made back to Cambridge, "and drifted together." Kids in the neighborhood often got together at different people's houses on Friday nights and danced. "Someone would have records," he said, "and someone would have a record player. We'd have soft drinks or lemonade if we had enough money."

Once they took a boat with their friend Atwood to James Island to hunt for Sitka deer, which are small. The three of them were going to walk into some thick underbrush, but my mother felt tired. While the others went on through the tall grass, she sat down—and landed right on one of the deer, which was hiding. She jumped up and screamed. The deer ran off but then stopped and stared back at her, since she was screaming so loudly. The two boys were laughing so hard they forgot to shoot the deer. After that, they called her "Deer Face." It sounds like a play on James Fenimore Cooper's Deerslayer, but it also sounds like "Dear Face."

My mother was a good shot, according to both Larry and Atwood. That was a big compliment, since they were life-long hunters and even kept shotguns in their lockers at school. My mother enjoyed going to the woods for target practice. She and her friend Ebbie, who would later be her maid of honor when she married my father, took turns shooting at unopened cans of tomatoes. If they hit them, the cans exploded with a red burst that looked like blood.

On another occasion, Larry and my mother took a ride on Atwood's airplane. "He flew right under the Choptank River Bridge," my mother told me. "Nearly scared us to death." After serving in the air corps during World War II, Atwood became a pilot for United Airlines.

Calvin, perhaps the real boyfriend who got away, became a bank clerk, like my father, and socialized with my parents when they moved back to Cambridge. My mother dated Calvin in 1943 and early 1944, probably while she was dating my father. She said, "I should have married Calvin" more than she did about any other former boyfriend.

Phil became a successful real estate agent and housing developer. He inherited money specifically bequeathed to allow him to travel to Africa each year and hunt. A restaurant he *owned, called The Point and located next to the Choptank River Bridge, had walls decorated with the mounted heads of kudu, oryx, Dall Sheep, Alpine Chamois, Hunter's Hartebeest, Isfahan Mouflan, and other wild animals, mostly exotic sheep and deer he had shot on his safaris.*

Near the end of her life, my mother got back in touch with Phil, who was worth a fortune. She called him at his home in Texas and struck up a phone friendship with the Latina woman who was acting as his companion. He helped my mother financially, paying off her maxed-out credit cards.

As a school girl, my mother was a promiscuous virgin, still proper despite the come-ons and teasing. But there was nothing she was more nostalgic about than necking, getting a tactile peek at sensuous possibilities, all glamour and no guilt, the excitement without the apprehension of pregnancy or disease, all rising action without a denouement. It left her, as well as her boyfriends, wanting more. With Carolyn, she could have that thrill again, but without the minuses. She could break the rules, flout the conventions, and not be a girl in trouble—at least not in the usual sense.

Three-Bedroom Apartment

The year when Carolyn and my mother moved back together, renting a three-bedroom apartment on Battery Lane, corresponded to the time when Carolyn's health began to deteriorate and their sexual (though not intimate) relationship had apparently come to an end. It was 1975, and they had progressed from living miles apart, after breaking up their household on Massachusetts Avenue, to living in apartments one on top of the other, so Carolyn could bang a broomstick on the ceiling and my mother could stomp on the floor if they wanted attention. It's odd that they decided to share their living quarters when their love life had diminished, almost as if the electricity they'd known was too dangerous and destructive. My mother became more of a care-giver, companion, and champion. She often told me that her favorite passage in the Bible was Corinthians 13:13, "And now abideth faith, hope, charity, these three; but the greatest of these is charity." So she devoted herself to Carolyn. It wasn't charity but caring, *caritas* in the sense of giving everything for the sake of love.

Still enamored, though, they exchanged love tokens, ripping a $2 bill in half, each keeping one of the pieces as a secret sign they belonged to each other. My mother gave Carolyn a gold filigree necklace with several pendants: a $2½ gold coin dated 1908, a gold hoop with the number 13 set in the middle, and a gold medallion of the Gemini twins—references to Carolyn's birthday of June 13. After Carolyn died, my mother wore the necklace herself.

Their move to the three-bedroom apartment also corresponded to the time when I was no longer living with them. I had transferred to Stony Brook University on Long Island, where I qualified for in-state tuition because my father lived in New York City. I was benefiting from the G.I. Bill, receiving monthly checks from the Veterans' Administration. I had found a girlfriend, a classmate in the Comparative Literature program, and spent the summer of 1975 in Manhattan, living with my father and stepmother in their apartment and working at RCA, punching figures about record-album sales into a computer, so I could see Vicki as often as possible. From then on, I would be a visitor when I saw my mother and Carolyn. I would be an outsider.

I can remember, though, when the decline became noticeable. We were returning from a visit to Captain Amos on the Eastern Shore, and we stopped for a late dinner at the Captain's Table, just west of the Chesapeake Bay Bridge. My mother's drink was an Old Fashioned, Carolyn's a Gibson. After a couple of rounds, the entrees of scallops and crab imperial arrived. Carolyn intoned, like some sort of tribal priestess, "With my hiatal hernia, I have to be careful how I swallow. But I know how to control it with my mental power. I just concentrate... like this." Almost immediately, however, she started choking and gasping. After my mother gave her some vigorous pats on the back, she managed to swallow or spit out a chunk of scallop—I can't remember which—but her face had turned red, her bug eyes were bulging more than usual, and she couldn't touch another bite. Her mental power had faltered, and it struck me that her health began to deteriorate alarmingly from that point on.

It wasn't just one ailment that plagued her, but a complex of medical problems, including aneurysms, high blood pressure, hyperglycemia, a degenerated spine, breathing difficulties, and obesity. Like my mother, she was a life-long smoker. She was still drinking cocktails every evening after 5:00, but she was also highly medicated. "She has a drawer full of pills," my mother told me, "one for her blood pressure, one to take the water out of her body, to take out the bloat, one so she won't be depressed, one to make her sleep."

Once, when I was sitting on her bedside, Carolyn said, "If I take these pills, my blood pressure will go up to 700."

"Why are you taking them then?" I asked.

"What do you want me to do, cough and break my aneurysms?"

Around this time, Carolyn's doctor diagnosed her condition as Cushing's Disease, and my mother recognized the symptoms, almost with gratitude that they explained so much about the course of Carolyn's life. She had a moon face, a "buffalo hump" between her shoulder blades, high blood pressure and blood sugar, brittle bones, weakness and fatigue, difficulty climbing stairs, trouble falling asleep, trouble paying attention, and especially decreased libido.

When I visited the apartment, Carolyn often reminisced about her singing career. She claimed that she was the first singer to give concerts in Newfoundland. When she was sitting in the dining car of a train, the waiter brought her a platter of moose meat. "The entire train gathered around my table," she said. "The moose was rare. It looked like a lump of coagulated blood. When they weren't looking, I threw it out the window."

Carolyn made fun of my mother for getting seasick on an ocean liner docked at a pier in New York harbor. She had grown up on the water, the daughter of an oysterman, and prided herself on being the only one of two thousand passengers who showed up in the dining room during a storm at sea. "You're hungry?" the waiter asked. "Always!" she said. "Bring on the first course!"

That story led her to repeat one she had told many times, about being naked with a ship's captain in his stateroom, how the steward interrupted them to deliver champagne while she was wearing a funeral wreath in her curly black hair. And with that story, she was back on tour, performing a recital of her hits.

She told us about getting off a train at dawn, with all her fans waiting, the photographers' flash bulbs going off. She told us about a flight through a blizzard when three of the plane's four engines caught on fire, forcing them to make an emergency landing, so she led the passengers in singing to keep them calm. She told us about cutting Mario Lanza's hair. She remembered how a tenor collapsed on stage, supposedly dead, and how she roared with laughter so hard she started crying because his penis had flopped out of his pants. "The critics thought I was weeping," she said. "They considered it my finest performance as an actress."

Her press releases had trumpeted that she was also an explorer and would have been an archaeologist if she hadn't become a singer, so she recounted the Smithsonian expedition that took her into the Yucatan in search of Mayan ruins. "I stepped into a whole nest of snakes," she said. "I could feel them striking up against my boots." She still had the machete she used to hack her way through the jungle, along with its leather sheath. When I was little, I was scared by her stories of digging out chiggers when they sat by the fire after setting up camp. She also collected Mayan folk songs from the natives, with the idea of performing them in her concerts.

"I can't stand listening to music anymore," she told me, "because I feel guilty." But she allowed me to put on a recording of John Dowland's lute songs, probably because "Come Again! Sweet Love Doth Now Invite" was one of the numbers she had performed in her concerts.

"This is so boring, if you've heard what I've heard," she said, going on to explain how the soprano "lets the connection fall on top of the hook and sings above the breath, like a choir boy." She demonstrated by singing a single, clear, high note.

"But you don't sound shrill like she does," I said.

"Yes, because I cover it. I put a lid on it. You have to feel lifted, like you're underwater. She doesn't give it enough height. The tone's too spread, when it should be up and down, a completely pure sound which has no sex."

When I played a recording of a tenor singing "If My Complaints," she said, "He's one of the boys, of course—you know what I mean. Trying to imitate the castrati."

I remembered how, when I was a boy soprano, Carolyn gave me some voice lessons and told me not to lift my head when I sang a higher note, but to look straight ahead and think about the note and the interval.

"The tone's too far back," she said. "It should be like a waterfall. He presses, so he'll have vibrato at the end. You sing down. That's what support is all about—keeping it down. When you tighten the tone, you feel little strings—palate up and face lifted."

Later, when the bass was singing, she laughed and said, "He's squeezing it out like a toothpaste tube! You should keep your jaw down. The tongue does all the pronunciation. Never spread your mouth when you're singing this kind of stuff."

It amazed me that even in her sickbed she could conduct a seminar.

Carolyn was very heavy, but she could make her own way to the bathroom if she pressed against the walls to keep herself upright. Even though she now spent most of her time in bed, Carolyn and my mother still had fights. If things became too heated, one of them phoned the police, who responded to the calls and told them to calm down and stay in their own bedrooms.

What did they fight about? They still harbored the same resentments, guilt, and insecurity. They traded recriminations. They worried about finances. "I never had enough money," my mother told me, "to do what I really wanted."

Carolyn used to put my mother down when she started "babbling," saying she was "tired of being around little minds." When my mother complained about something that Carolyn considered insignificant, she told her, "You make little problems into the Empire State Building." When my mother fussed over something, Carolyn said, "See what I have to put up with? You give me orders 24 hours a day and make me a five-year-old."

My mother, of course, got fed up that the woman who depended on her could treat her like that and could say "At least I've been somebody!"

"I've got to move," my mother told me. "I've got to do something. I've got to think of myself for once. But she's got her good points. It's hard to forget her kindnesses over the years. You see, I remember what she used to be."

She told me that Carolyn wouldn't throw away *anything*. "It's almost a fetish with her. She even saves pill bottles. You see, she's afraid she'll be left with nothing, so she lets things clutter up. When she's away, sometimes I weed out as much as I can. She won't notice anything's missing for months. If she asks where something is, I just say, 'I don't know.' But I'd hate like hell to let her down, because in her own way she's been a good friend." So my mother, in the course of one monologue, could shift her position from moving out, like Nora in *A Doll's House,* to staying put.

Soon after renting the three-bedroom apartment, my mother quit her bookkeeping job at Community Auto. She hated the way they treated her like a nobody, and she missed feeling special, as she had at the bank, so she started seeking other opportunities. After passing a test, she tried to find a job as a social worker in Prince George's County, but she didn't get beyond a single interview. She applied for positions as a teller, explaining in her letters that banking was in her blood. I'm not sure why she didn't return to the Bank of Bethesda, but maybe she couldn't. Maybe they were aware of her petty larceny, how she took a $20 bill from Earlene's cash drawer occasionally, or maybe her transgressions were more serious than that, and Mr. Sacks told her she was free to go but not to come back. But I imagine that she was still enraged at the gender discrimination, the unequal pay, and refused to return on principle. She and Carolyn considered moving to Annapolis or to Bethany Beach, where they had the chance to buy a house near the ocean, but no job offers came. Their projects for getting away all fizzled out. They almost bought a VW camper equipped with a kitchenette, two couches that converted to bunks, and a toilet, but they backed out because they felt the salesman had lied to them about the terms. So my mother swallowed her pride, ate some more of that peck of dirt, and returned to Community Auto for another four years of listening to coarse language and being ignored.

During the twelve years they lived in that apartment, I married my girlfriend from Stony Brook, got divorced when she discovered that she was a lesbian (an interesting coincidence), and became involved with a redhead who would become my second wife (and eventually my second ex-wife). My mother couldn't understand why I didn't marry girls who were more like her. In between those marriages, I reverted to being a spoiled, surly boy when I returned home for a visit—but I was *their* boy, so they indulged me and fussed over me and put up with my moods. Once, for some stupid reason I've forgotten, I got so mad that I kicked a hole in the decorative red contact paper my mother had applied to the back of Carolyn's upright piano, which jutted out into the middle of the third bedroom. My mother loved to repair things, but the hole never got fixed. The simple solution was to push the piano against a wall so the damage I'd inflicted wouldn't show.

My mother quit her job at Community Auto for a second and final time in 1979, taking early retirement when she was 55 years old. She still had a job, though, or maybe it was a religious vocation: taking care of Carolyn.

Ruth Small, Carolyn's classmate from the Peabody Conservatory, made it possible. She became their benefactor, providing them with a check every month. How many singers are lucky enough to have a patron, especially *after* their singing careers are over? My mother used her bookkeeping expertise to give Ruth detailed accounts of their monthly expenditures and estimate how much they would require the following month. She also let her know when and why they needed to buy something expensive, like a new car, and Ruth graciously allocated the funds.

Eventually, when she had to serve as executor of Carolyn's estate, my mother destroyed almost all of her correspondence to keep it from prying eyes, but she kept a letter from Ruth in its envelope and stored it in a tin reserved for treasures. Written in the 1930s, it looks like a love letter, a testament to a schoolgirl crush that became a life-long devotion. It reads, in part:

> I hope you will remember, whatever happens, that I have loved you for 2 years as a servant loves his master, as a dog loves his master—and now I can say that I love you no more in the old way but what joy I found in looking into your eyes last nite! I am so indebted to you. You helped me find myself in life.
>
> You are very strange and exotic and I think you are swell, but I'm scared to death of you—I will come over soon again to talk to you if I get up the nerve.

Ruth's maiden name was Behrend, and when she sent Carolyn a Christmas card, she signed it "Bare end."

Ruth's husband, Colonel Small, was in charge of the USO, so they knew Bob Hope and arranged for Elizabeth Taylor to appear at the Arts Club of Washington, of which they were active members and probably donors. Carolyn's last public appearance occurred when she introduced my cousin Dail, her voice student, before a song recital at the Arts Club.

Ruth's son Hal had progressed from playing organ with his rock group, The Lunatic Fringe, to performing piano recitals of Bach's *Goldberg Variations* and Mussorgsky's *Pictures at an Exhibition*. Now going by the name he shared with his father, Haskell Small, he also composed his own works for solo piano, chamber ensembles, and orchestras, including several songs for sopranos.

It amazes me that Ruth never acted jealous, never seemed to think of my mother as her rival for Carolyn's affections. But after the two of them became the beneficiaries of Ruth's largesse, they were highly suspicious of Colonel Small's protégé and artistic project, a musician named Tomchek, whom they considered a poseur and suspected was a con-man.

I gave a poetry reading with Ruth's daughter, Sherry Small Sundick, at the Arts Club, using the occasion to read "Soprano," a poem about Carolyn and her adventures. A long-lined, Whitmanic celebration of her singing career, it declared, "No one believes your stories, but all are true."

Now, in her late sixties, an invalid who struggled to get up and lumber her way to the bathroom, Carolyn told me about a wonder drug she had discovered in a tabloid. "It keeps your cells from dying," she said. "I might be revitalized by the stuff and go back on stage."

When Carolyn was frazzled with anxiety, she lifted her hands in front of her own face, close but not touching, moving them gently, as if washing away the worries like so much dirt, and then wringing them out, shaking off the imaginary moisture. "There," she said, "*finito*." She liked to say she was "throwing out her nerves." The method is similar to Japanese *reiki*, in which healing fingers hover just above the flesh to massage the person's aura.

Sometimes, when my mother was troubled, Carolyn said, "Bobby, let me help," and performed the ritual for her. If nothing else, it was an effective psychological ploy. And part of it may have been the sensual excitement of almost touching, a suspense that remained suspended, like a promise or an I.O.U.

Some evenings, my mother still crawled into Carolyn's bed to cuddle and have her back scratched. I remember pausing in the hall to watch them through the open door, always grateful for peace between them. They could still act lovey-dovey, and Carolyn still complimented Bobby on her appearance.

"Those shoes look pretty on your little feet," she said one afternoon, when my mother had dressed to go out on some errand.

"Thank you," she replied. "The bows are sticking up."

My mother served as paid companion, nurse, and financial manager, still pretending that the two of them were cousins. But it was a commitment based on love, and not a "love thy neighbor" attachment, no matter how sisterly they acted. Victorians would call it a "Boston marriage," which the *Oxford English Dictionary* defines as a term "used euphemistically to refer to the cohabitation of two women, esp. in a romantic relationship or intimate friendship."

Disclosure #16

Bobby and Carolyn both attended the poetry reading I gave at the Arts Club of Washington in January 1982, and they heard my poem about Carolyn, "Soprano":

    Can you still believe it—your flowery gowns,
    a steamer trunk of glossies, press kits, raves from long-gone daily
        rags,
    cameras popping when you swaggered off the Pullman car at
        dawn?
    Can you believe the stir before the burial at sea?
    When a steward knocked on the stateroom door,
    you and the captain, buck naked, clinked tumblers in his rumpled
        bunk,
    a funeral wreath haloed in your ringlets.

    No one believes your stories, but all are true:
    trimming the pompadour of Mario Lanza, presenting a baton—
    Ormandy's gift when you dubbed in a part—to a patient who
        conducted to a record,
    dancing in the White House, where the Vice President pinched
        your rear.
    When a prop conked out on the airplane, ice on the wings over
        Wyoming,
    you led the passengers in singing, insisting on four-part harmony.
    Once down through the blizzard, you breezed on stage with your
        luggage,
    flung your fur coat on the Steinway, and began an Italian air.

    Little remains—your life on the road long over
    and you back in Maryland, the tidewater inlets where your father
        tonged for oysters—
    but nothing lets you go. You pencil on eyebrows, you pencil a
        blurry line
    on the vodka bottle—someone's been cutting it with water.
    Nothing can be trusted: your arteries mined,
    your broken back still not knitting, your bones dissolving.
    You press your hands on the hallway walls and edge
    toward the toilet, but your feet lag behind, as if stuck,
    and you collapse, enormous, still muscle-bound from singing.

When you hacked through the Yucatan, digging out chiggers
and jotting down Mayan folk tunes, what were you after?
When you married a Marine who stormed Iwo Jima,
who captured a flag with a rising sun, whose letters were full of
    volcanic ash—
then dropped him for a cowboy, punching cattle on the ranges of
    Cuba,
what in the *world* were you after?
A lover who shot himself, a patron who left you stranded in Milan,
a tenor whose cock flopped out when he swooned on stage:
your laughter was taken for weeping, your greatest performance.

Pieces, nothing but pieces—a crossword puzzle
you're too bored to finish. Nothing matters, nothing
is ever worth a damn, can you believe no more than that?
If so, you're ready to believe anything:
the truth of commercials, the testimony of headlines—
"Top Docs Predict: Scientific Proof of an Afterlife."

In the life before, in Barcelona,
dust from the curtain almost choked you when it rose,
but you went on anyway—*Remember me, but ah, forget my fate.*
Now, you take it personally. What can I say
that won't hurt your feelings, since everything hurts,
a brusque reminder, and silence is unbearable
as the songs you hate to hear,
preferring talk shows on the radio as you sleep?
Cover your ears—and it just gets louder.
Open your mouth—and the world is all ovation, all applause.
Whether you like it or not, it makes you sing.

Vissi d'arte, vissi d'amore

I never expected my mother to move back to Cambridge, Maryland. I figured that the break was permanent, that she was glad she'd fled from the gossip, the "small-minded people" who had judged her. But when Carolyn's health deteriorated and she needed to go into a nursing home, that's where they went.

Their patron, Ruth Small, continued to support them with remarkable generosity, sending my mother a monthly check that covered the rent for an apartment, grocery bills, utilities, and other expenses, which my mother carefully enumerated like the bookkeeper she had been. When Ruth died, she bequeathed my mother an annuity of $1,000 a month that helped her survive—without moving in with me and my family. It was a blessing that we were not forced to live together. As much as I loved my mother, we were both difficult, prone to quarrels, mutually demanding, quick to "press each other's buttons" by saying something inflammatory, by wallowing in our grudges from the past.

My mother's life, back in Cambridge, revolved around the Mallard Bay nursing home, where she became close friends with Susan Wingate, one of the nurses. Susan lived down county in a house on the waterfront in Madison. Sadie, my mother's mother, had grown up there, and my mother liked being able to return to her roots when the Wingates invited her to dinner.

"Bobby brought that little bit of class you don't see now," Susan told me. "She knew about fine art, things we weren't exposed to here. She played music in Carolyn's room all the time. They were like sisters. They teased and picked at each other."

My mother took Carolyn on rides in her wheelchair and got her to activities, such as making Christmas ornaments and coloring Easter eggs. "Carolyn would get bored if Bobby wasn't here," Susan said. "She took her outside and down the street and didn't sign her out."

Carolyn had the first private room off the lobby. My mother got a small air-conditioner and had a man remove the bottom pane from the window so he could install it. "The administrator had a fit," Susan said. "They had it out in the middle of the lobby." I knew how fierce a defender my mother could be, so I'm sure the argument was loud and passionate, at least on her part. And I know that the air-conditioner stayed where it was.

Susan's daughter was a teenager who volunteered at the nursing home. People told Carolyn that she liked to sing but nobody could get her to do it, so when Chrissy was taking care of her rounds one day and entered the room, Carolyn, propped up in her bed, shouted "Begin!" Chrissy began to sing at the foot of her bed, probably afraid to keep quiet after that trained operatic voice had boomed out. It was almost certainly the last lesson Carolyn ever gave.

Once my mother had donated Carolyn's press clippings and concert programs to the Peabody Conservatory, she began agitating for some sort of recognition. In 1988, the director of the conservatory attended a ceremony in the nursing home and presented Miss Long with the Director's Recognition Award "for her distinguished career in music."

I wasn't able to attend the gala, but the lounge was packed with friends, cousins, nurses, sitters, and patients. Carolyn wore a long red gown, with a corsage pinned on, her hair beautifully coiffed with flourishes of gray at the temples, and sat in a padded armchair next to a Chippendale secretary. The citation that the director recited began by quoting from raves in newspaper reviews. It went on to say, "Obviously the critics loved you, Carolyn Creighton Long, for your career spanned many years of successful performances, one after another, until you retired to assist young singers on their road to a singing career." It mentioned that her "beautiful voice and charming manner inspired many aspiring sopranos, including the Director of Alumni Relations, who remembered her as 'the most glamorous, exciting woman I had ever met.'" It applauded her as a "real trooper" who "averaged about 100 concerts a year, logging 32,000 miles your first year alone, and you never missed a performance."

Andrew, the care-giver who accompanied Carolyn on occasional trips when she was well enough to go out, took a video of the occasion, and I'm amused by how flustered, fidgety, and buoyant with pride my mother was, making sure everything was as festive as possible. It was her day as much as Carolyn's.

She had devoted many years to taking care of her longtime companion, first in the three-bedroom apartment they shared and then in the nursing home. She visited daily and hung around the place. When she couldn't be there, she hired sitters to keep Carolyn company and attend to her needs. She made sure people treated her friend and "cousin"—the love of her life—like a star.

So it's odd that my mother was having her hair done at a beauty parlor in Trappe, early in the morning, when Carolyn died in the hospital on the riverside, the same one where my mother had given birth to me. Carolyn had been back in intensive care for weeks, away from the nursing home, and it hadn't appeared she would ever be well enough to leave. When I asked my mother about the cause of death, she said, "Sepsis. Carrie's whole body was chock-full of infection." It made me think of septic tanks, and I felt sorry for Carolyn, my surrogate parent, but even sorrier for my mother.

I returned to Cambridge for the memorial service in October 1991. The day before, my mother and I drove to Dorchester Memorial Park, just off Route 50 on the way to Ocean City, to view the grave site. When we pulled up and got out of the car, I burst out laughing. Immediately to the left of Carolyn's marker stood another with a family name engraved in large capital letters: "BOOZE." It struck me as funny that someone so fond of drinking and gaiety would end up with a sign denoting liquor right next door.

Besides her name and her birth and death dates, Carolyn's marker had an inscription in Italian followed by a treble-clef sign:

CAROLYN CREIGHTON LONG
1915-1991
"PACE, PACE MIO DIO" 𝄞

In a cemetery, "Peace, peace my God" makes devotional sense, although Carolyn wasn't very religious. The line, of course, comes from an aria in Verdi's *La Forza del Destino*, one of Carolyn's favorite recital pieces, her big number. She had even named one of her dogs "Pace."

"Look at the other side," my mother told me. On the back of the granite marker with a rough-hewn top, my mother's name appeared with her birth date and a hyphen:

CAROLYN BAYLY DRURY
1924-

"Isn't that a little ghoulish?" I asked.

Ever practical, my mother was economizing by purchasing one marker for both of them and making good use of the plot Carolyn's parents had bequeathed. But above all it was a statement. My mother had often told me, "I don't want to be buried in the Christ Church graveyard," which was where most of her ancestors were buried. "If you put me there, I'll haunt you forever."

Carolyn's epitaph could have been "VISSI D'ARTE, VISSI D'AMORE," the aria she sang as Tosca when she performed the role in a concert version of the opera with the Austin Symphony. Indeed, she lived for art and lived for love. But my mother chose the inscription, and "PACE, PACE MIO DIO" referred to God, so it fit more decorously into a cemetery.

My mother sent Carolyn's obituary to many newspapers, from the home-town *Daily Banner* to the Baltimore *Sun* and the Washington *Post*, all of which published it, but for some reason the tireless promoter of her longtime companion could not get up the nerve to submit it to *Opera News*. I think she was afraid that the magazine might decide that Carolyn Long's passing didn't merit their notice. Later, she regretted her timidity, as though it represented an act of betrayal.

But I have been studying the obituaries in *Opera News*, and I believe the magazine would have welcomed Carolyn, first as a tribute to her many performances in the Metropolitan Opera's summer season in 1948 at the Cincinnati Zoo, second because of the Gershwin Festival tour conducted by a young Lorin Maazel, third because of hundreds of song recitals when she was part of Columbia Artists Management's Community Concert series, fourth because of her singing in Eugene Ormandy's recording of Honegger's *Jeanne d'Arc au bûcher*, fifth because of her performance as Tosca with the Austin Symphony under Ezra Rachlin. She earned that attention, that applause, and my mother worked hard to keep her name alive. Erotic love had culminated in devotion. What had seemed like an on-again, off-again affair had grown to resemble a hard-earned marriage. Grief would become the motive power of my mother's remaining years.

Disclosure #17

My friend from the army, John Walker, helped me move my mother and her Siamese cat, Aida, in a rented van from Cambridge to Cincinnati in 2001, ten years after Carolyn's death. When we stopped overnight at a motel in Pennsylvania, we transferred her from the cab of the van to the distant room by having her stand on the luggage rack on wheels and hold the rod above her head, like a commuter on a crowded bus, as we pushed her down the long corridor.

The next day, after we had unloaded her furniture and boxes into her ground-floor apartment, not far from my house in Cincinnati, John took me aside and put a hand on my shoulder. "Be kind," he said. "I know it won't always be easy."

Exile in Cincinnati

Although my mother was having serious medical and financial troubles, she moved to Cincinnati to be close to me and her two grandchildren, Eric and Becky. She wanted them to call her "Granny Gus," but I asked, "Do you really think that's a good idea?" The name made me picture an unshaven bartender, cigar in hand, wearing a frilly gingham dress. My mother was supposed to be a boy when she was born, but there was nothing especially masculine about Bobby, except that she liked to fix things with tools. She pondered the question for a minute and then said, "Well, how about 'Granny Goose'?" They ended up calling her Granny.

She first told me she wanted to be a grandmother when I was nine or ten. It's interesting that once she had Eric to dote on, she used one of Carolyn's pet expressions and told him, "You're my eyeballs!" While adopting her friend's lingo, she was also paying tribute. When we took her to the zoo, I pushed her around in her wheelchair, blonde-haired Becky sitting in her lap. "Don't take me to see the monkeys," she said. "They always pee on me."

People thought my mother was a character. When she had an appointment with Dr. Powell, a tall, balding family-practice physician who wore Looney Tunes ties, she brought a list of health concerns she wanted to discuss. There were always at least half a dozen ailments:

>   Back pain—excruciating!
>   Breathing difficulties—my COPD
>   Lack of appetite
>   Toenails need clipping
>   Trouble sleeping
>   Bum knees—giving out

"Now Carolyn," he said, "I've got other patients. You have to limit yourself to one or two items."

She looked exasperated. "Dr. Powell," she said, "I'm an old woman, and I'm in constant pain. There's a hell of a lot wrong with me. I'm falling apart. It wouldn't hurt you to prescribe something that might improve my disposition."

He laughed, because she was so ornery and such a "character." She might complain about her emphysema one minute and her itchiness the next. He gave her prescriptions for inhalers and antihistamines. "Don't you have any free samples around this place?" she said, and he often came back with a bag full. But he was skittish about prescribing narcotics, probably nervous about lawsuits, so he referred her to a pain clinic where she could get prescriptions of morphine and Oxycontin, as well as epidural steroid injections in her spine.

After she underwent a biopsy of her right lung, the surgeon told her the good news that it wasn't cancer. But smoking had really done a number on her lungs. The alveoli were damaged, and air wasn't able to circulate in and out properly. It was getting trapped in the air sacs, so exhaling was especially difficult. She had also aspirated a good deal of food, but he'd cleaned out what he could. She had to go on oxygen, full-time.

"It was easier for me to give up drinking than smoking," my mother told me, "and Lord knows I loved my sody pops." I remembered the wooden cigarette-pack dispenser that hung on our kitchen wall in a succession of apartments on Battery Lane, with a poem that began "Tobacco is a dirty weed—I like it" attached to the front.

An oxygen machine, several tall canisters that looked like fire extinguishers, small ones that looked like fat thermos bottles, and a portable oxygen kit soon arrived at her apartment. Whenever we went out to a store or a restaurant or an opera or a doctor's appointment, she needed both the wheelchair and the portable oxygen machine. It limited how far she could travel, so it no longer seemed feasible to return to Cambridge for a vacation, although we could have carried a supply of extra canisters. Even after she had started depending on oxygen, I found packs of Merit cigarettes she had hidden in various drawers. I sympathized with all of the health problems that plagued her, but the breathing was what worried me.

She had often said, "I always wanted to be an old woman," but she hated feeling so bad. She recoiled against being an invalid, so she leaned against the stove, with the walker around her, and cooked pot roasts with potatoes, onions, and carrots in a kettle she had salvaged from the bay house. Then she called me up and said, "Your supper's ready," although I had no idea she was making dinner for my family.

One day, when my mother was recuperating in a nursing home after a stay in the hospital, I entered her apartment and found Mary, the housekeeper who also worked on the clean-up crew of the apartment complex, rushing from the bedroom, flustered, her face red and breaking into a sweat. My mother wasn't able to get to the front door if anyone knocked, so she had given several people, including Mary, keys to her apartment. But Mary didn't need to be there while my mother was away, so I was suspicious, but we didn't find out why until my mother returned and discovered, detective that she was, that her two diamond rings were missing. My friend LaWanda guessed that Mary must have stolen and pawned them and probably went to the nearest shop. When we visited the American Trading Company, LaWanda spotted the rings in the display counter. We brought my mother back to the store, and she identified them and said what they were worth, according to the appraisal of a jeweler in Cambridge. They were on sale for a quarter of that value.

"I'll sell them back to you for what I gave her," the dealer said, "but I can't do any better than that. You'll have to take legal action for the rest." But when we asked if he would be a witness, he declined, explaining that he didn't want to be involved because it would hurt business and she might take action against him.

So we bought back the rings and my mother left a message for Mary, telling her not to come back. "You know why," she said. But it seemed like too much trouble to sue.

My mother's bedroom was a shrine for Carolyn, with pictures on the walls and two large boxes of Carolyn's memorabilia, including two binders of photocopied press clippings, under the bed. She also had a bookcase dedicated to my own publications. She couldn't resist being my archivist too.

"Not a day goes by I don't think of Carolyn," she said. But she told me that she had messed up her life and made a big mistake getting together with Carolyn. She begged me not to mess up mine the same way.

Once, when my mother was telling me about one of the visiting nurses who had come to her apartment earlier that day, she remarked, "I think she may be queer."

In years past, I wouldn't have said a thing, but I wanted her to be more open about herself, so I forced the issue and said, "It takes one to know one."

"I didn't love women," she replied, calmly. "I just loved one woman."

Disclosure #18

"If you ever want a rest, don't go to a nursing home," my mother said. "They go by all the time in the hallway. They come in with papers, activities for the day. They're all crooks. They yell back and forth like they're in a ball field." She hated it when she wasn't well enough to stay in her own apartment and had to move into the Western Hills Retirement Village.

The room she shared was pleasant but institutional: maroon carpet, beige walls with a brown border near the ceiling, seashells on the paper strip, and a flowered curtain over Venetian blinds. In the hallway, there was a chair with a scale above its backrest so a patient could get weighed while sitting down. In the lounge, there was an electric organ with pedals. On the bulletin board, there were signs for "Split the Pot," "Moonlight Ball," "Ice Cream Social," and "Love Is Ageless." Around the nurses' station, the floors were polished to a glow that made the wood look watery.

Her bed was near the door, not the window, but she didn't seem to care. Using her checkbook, I bought a new dresser, a television, and an easy chair for visitors. I also hammered in a couple of nails and hung up a painting of her Siamese cat and the framed front cover of a magazine with a beautiful photograph of Carolyn Long. But it wasn't much compared to the decorating my mother did in Carolyn's room back at Mallard Bay.

She was rebellious from the start, scorning and shunning the nursing home's activities: sing-a-longs, spelling bees, bingo, trivia, Yahtzee, cheese & sparkling juice socials, ice cream parties, rosary making, bible chapel, mass, Lawrence Welk on TV, old-time carnivals, exercise, making pizzas, making donut holes, taking a trip to see baby animals at Sunrock Farm, playing spin the bottle. She refused to go to the dining room for any of her meals. *"I don't want to be around those old people,"* she said. *"They drool. They fall asleep with their mouths open. You can't have a decent conversation with any of them, not a single one."*

Give All to Love

My life resembles my mother's most closely in giving all to love, as Emerson advises, obeying my heart. When I was married to my second wife, I was secretly despondent about our relationship, its intimate limits and constraints, the depressing distances between us. Like my mother, I acted on a passionate impulse when I put my hands on the shoulders of LaWanda, a friend I had known for over fifteen years, then touched her cheeks and began kissing her. She had come to our house and was crying, drinking a gin and tonic, sitting alone in the upstairs den after my wife had gone out to a bar with another girlfriend without asking her to join them. I had met LaWanda at a party during my first year in Cincinnati and was immediately attracted, but I held back because she was married, because I had a girlfriend (who was spending the year in Provincetown and would later become my second wife), and because she seemed unreachably beautiful. Her wild hair was the first thing I noticed, but there was an openness in her face, a smile that was sensual but innocent. I had a crush, and part of it derived from our shared affinities for poetry and the music of Bach. I had wanted to make advances for years but held back because I was afraid that LaWanda would reject me. It took me a long time to find the nerve to act on something so serious that it would break up my own family, as mine had been broken up. The cause was the same: giving all for erotic love. And LaWanda was more like my mother than any of my previous wives or girlfriends: passionate, high-strung, brilliant, and generous. If Carolyn Long had met her, she would have "loved her to pieces" and insisted on giving her a voice lesson on the spot. What I thought at first was an affair turned out to be permanent, a marriage of true minds and bodies, with all of the volatility of the relationship my mother shared with Carolyn.

While I was attending a family reunion with my wife and children, LaWanda spent time visiting my mother in her apartment, bringing her things she needed from the grocery store as well as little gifts like marzipan fruit and a teapot in the shape of a cat. As usual, my mother was prying, probably suspicious and certainly nosy, and asked her what was going on between us.

"John's more my friend than she is," LaWanda said. "Can I tell you something? We're in love."

"Have you slept together?"

"Yes."

"I'm so happy," she said, "I could get up and dance a jig!" Since my mother needed a wheelchair to get around, that exclamation was especially emphatic. She started calling LaWanda her "secret daughter-in-law."

But it wasn't long before my mother became ambivalent, counseling me to think of the children, since they came first. "Don't make the same mistakes I did," she said. She was interfering again, so I didn't get divorced and remarried until five years later, soon after her death. "I don't think you would have ever married me," LaWanda said, "if your mother was still alive." I had to concede that she was probably right.

My mother's advice about sticking it out in the old marriage was a compound of jealousy, pragmatism, hypocrisy, and what Alfred Doolittle, the dustman in *My Fair Lady*, would call "middle-class morality." Like all of my wives and girlfriends, LaWanda loomed as a rival. My mother always wondered why I couldn't find a girl who was more like her, even though LaWanda was clearly her match. It's true that Vicki, my first wife, shared her sexual preference, but they were at odds as long as that marriage lasted. It wasn't until we were divorced and Vicki was openly lesbian that she wrote my mother a note addressing her as "Mom."

"Carolyn predicted it," my mother said. "She could tell she was queer from the first time she laid eyes on her. And one time Vicki turned her big brown eyes on me, and I had my own suspicions." My mother also talked about people who "accused" her of being homosexual. "No, we're not," she'd laugh. "We're cousins, we come from the same hometown, and she's my dearest friend. We've been through a lot together."

My mother confided in LaWanda in ways she could never bring herself to confide in me. When they were talking in her apartment, my mother pointed out a silver bowl filled with artificial fruit. "I was so mad when Carolyn bought it," she said. "She spent $250! That was a lot of money in those days." She picked up a wax banana my daughter Becky liked to play with, pretending it was a telephone, chatting into it, and told LaWanda that she and Carolyn had used it, along with dabs of Vaseline, in their intimate relations—as definitive an admission of her sexuality as my mother ever made. She also said that once, when I was a boy, I saw her whittling the tip of the banana with a paring knife to smooth out the rough edges.

I was happy for this evidence of her intimacy with Carolyn. It struck me as funny, sweet, and very human that they had enjoyed a sex toy. My mother was clearly obsessed with sex, although she hadn't enjoyed having it with my father, describing his performances as "rough and fast," but also complaining that he frequently carried a magazine into the bathroom so he could masturbate. It's not surprising that her stock opening and conversational ice-breaker was "How's your love life?"

Disclosure #19

One day, I asked my mother why Carolyn had divorced her two husbands, Blair and Duke. She frowned, shook her head, and nodded toward her roommate Dorothy, who was sitting by the window, under an embroidered cross her children had put on the wall. I had already noticed that Dorothy's family didn't come daily, as I did, but when they came they stayed longer. I remembered a nurse, one my mother didn't like, telling Dorothy, "I swear, you look forty years younger today. I'm not lying." Nothing sounds falser that someone who insists, "I'm not lying." But Dorothy beamed, delighted by the compliment.

Later on, after a nurse had wheeled Dorothy out of the room to take her to some activity in the lounge, my mother looked at me and said, "Pencil dicks." I laughed, because I knew exactly what she meant, that Carolyn's ex-husbands, one a Marine lieutenant colonel, the other a cowboy, weren't well enough endowed to satisfy her. She had delayed answering my question until we were alone. My mother was still sharp, still cagey enough to wait until giving me the bawdy news.

I always thought she could have been a detective, partly because she liked to snoop around. She confessed that when she stayed in a motel room she listened to what the people next door were saying by placing a drinking glass on the wall and putting her ear to the makeshift amplifier. But her real investigative gift lay in her powers of observation.

In the nursing home, she was still sharp enough to catch the careless mistakes some of the attendants made. "I looked around," she said, "and spied that they hadn't locked the bed when they brought it in. I noticed that when no one else did. I'm very astute." She paused. "I've always been astute."

What Really Happened

One day in the nursing home, I asked my mother how she and Carolyn had met. They'd been acquainted for a long time, but Carolyn was nine years older and moved in a different circle, which my mother considered a "fast crowd." One of her high-school pals in our hometown was Bernice Frankel, whose father owned a department store. Carolyn gave her singing lessons before she went into show business and changed her name to Bea Arthur. It annoyed my mother that even though Bernice, as she always called her, was Carolyn's age, the almanac listed a birth year that made her even younger than *she* was.

"Carolyn was in the little children's room at Sunday School," my mother said, thinking of when they really got to know each other in 1956. "I was in a room with big kids. She said *'Basta!'* to make the Boy Scouts in the next room be quiet. We looked at each other. I said, 'Hello, Carolyn, how are you,' and shook hands with her. With her makeup on, she was one of the most beautiful women I ever saw. It wasn't natural beauty."

My father had known Carolyn for some time before that meeting of the two women in church. He took voice lessons with her, and they both sang in a variety show she directed at the state mental hospital, where he and Carolyn performed "Singin' in the Rain" together. My mother said, "Phil had lessons with her any time he could—at her house, where she had a piano, a Knabe. She always wanted a grand piano and a *Grove's Dictionary of Music*. Never got either. And she wanted to go to Ireland. Your father got involved with Carolyn first."

She told me that Captain Amos and Nellie, Carolyn's parents, took a rich man's boat down the Intracoastal Waterway to Florida and left their Buick in Cambridge. When they got back in the new year, which was 1958, Nellie was barely alive. "Carolyn," my mother said, "I think a dying woman just went in your house." The mother she adored had bone cancer.

"Then she died, and there was a horribly big funeral," my mother told me. "I sat with Carolyn and her family and got criticized for that. Phil was with us too. Carolyn never cried. They say you shouldn't cry. I'm not very dignified. I cry. Not in front of people, they say.

"So Carolyn was lonesome. We said, 'Come by and stay at our house. You can sleep on the sofa in the living room.' She came and we started looking at television, which was all snow. And then... what happens on a sofa... happened.

"She was going out there in the kitchen and making pies almost every night, apple pies. There was sugar and flour on the floor every morning. I didn't know her well enough to correct her. She couldn't get to sleep, so she made pies. We were both in our room, asleep. You had moved upstairs, and she was in your old room. So everyone had their own rooms.

"Carolyn liked most anything on TV, especially cowboy pictures. I drank Coca-Cola and I.W. Harper. Carolyn drank almost anything, but she couldn't drink Scotch.

"Everywhere Carolyn went, someone wanted to have an affair with her. A girl who sang in the choir—she came from Easton, I think, maybe to take voice lessons—put her arm around Carolyn while I was making something in the kitchen. I heard Carolyn say, 'No, not here.'"

I remembered that when we were living on Massachusetts Avenue, another voice student, Ruth Pitts, had a case on Carolyn and they had an affair. One day, they called me into Carolyn's studio in the living room and made an announcement: "Guess what? Ruth may be our cousin!" Even then, as a teenager, I knew what that meant. They might be involved with her sexually.

"Everybody Carolyn knew," my mother said, "was in love with her."

It made sense that my mother remembered everything about that period so clearly. It was the dramatic climax of her life—or at least the turning point. Everything was heightened and had taken on a glow. I had never heard these stories before, but they came out so easily and sounded right. I was sorry I had never asked before.

"Carolyn was embarrassed," my mother said, "about something in that poem you wrote about her."

"You mean 'Soprano'?"

"Not all of her stories were true. You know how she told everyone she sang in the first English opera in Spain?"

"Yes, Purcell's *Dido and Aeneas*. That was in Barcelona."

"Well, she got there for the dress rehearsal, and there was so much dust on the ancient curtain of the theatre that when it rose it almost choked her—like you said. But then she got sick and went back to Italy and never returned for the actual performances. Kurt Weinholt of Columbia Artists was so mad he severed their relationship, voided her contract. I had the letter he sent her but I burned it, literally set it on fire with Carolyn's lighter and dropped it in the ashtray. Her patron got tired of Carolyn having a good time in Italy, so she cut her off without a cent. And there she was, stranded in a foreign country with no money, no job. Her father had to wire her enough to come home."

"Poor Carrie," I said.

When Carolyn was diagnosed with Cushing's Disease in the 1980s, my mother was sure that it explained the abrupt decline of her singing career. The other reasons were too depressing and demeaning to consider. Laziness?

Loss of nerve? Lack of interest? Drinking? Vocal troubles? Bad luck? People who let her down? No, the medical excuse was the one my mother believed. My own sense is that Carolyn risked her career by taking time off, at the height of her success, to learn roles that would propel her into the big time of opera. She wasn't satisfied with minor parts, or even important ones in concert performances of dramatic works, like the lead in *Tosca* with the Austin Symphony. She was tired of the endless touring, herself and her gay accompanists on the Community Concert circuit, following or just ahead of the von Trapp Family, giving so much of herself every night. She had the voice, but she lost the bet. It ended with the nervous breakdown that brought her back to her hometown and into our cottage on William Street.

Disclosure #20

Over the years, the name "Marnie" kept coming up, especially on evenings when my mother and Carolyn started to probe and poke at each other (I called it "sniping"), becoming suspicious and jealous as they drank, on alert for the resumption of hostilities. Marnie had apparently shared an apartment with Carolyn in New York. "She went to all of Carolyn's concerts," my mother said, exaggerating as usual. "I spotted her at Constitution Hall when Carolyn sang the **Magnificat.** *"*

Marnie, it was clear, was my mother's rival. After Carolyn had returned from Italy and my father had started taking voice lessons with her, my mother saw Marnie for the first time at the Yacht Club, sitting at a table next to Carolyn.

"Marnie was short," my mother said in the nursing home. "Curly hair, right cute looking. I think they were lovers, but Carolyn didn't talk about it. While Nellie was dying, Marnie came down. Carolyn didn't know where to go. She was afraid Marnie would get mad. So we all slept in the hospital. One of us would stay up and the other two would sleep, one on the bed with Carolyn's mother." It was the beginning of 1958, and my mother suspected that Carolyn was still involved with Marnie. She knew that the two of them had spent a weekend together on Fire Island, after which my mother met Carolyn in New York City and they got a hotel room. I'm not sure what I was doing, but it may have been one of the times when I stayed with my grandmother Sadie.

Crossing the Choptank River Bridge, driving north into Talbot County, where the liquor laws were more relaxed, was liberating for my mother. I have a hunch that it also served as a sanctuary of erotic freedom, away from the gossip and prying of Cambridge, Maryland.

She and Carolyn went to movies at the drive-in theatre on Route 50 near Trappe. They spent a lot of time in Oxford, at the waterfront home of Margaret Carreau, whose songs Carolyn performed during her recitals. They weren't exactly art songs, but there was a market then for pieces a singer trained in opera could perform, something like Mario Lanza's "Be My Love." While my mother and Carolyn were drinking cocktails with Margaret on the screen porch, I played catch with myself among the shade trees. It was a challenge trying to collect the falling baseball in my mitt as it was diverted by branches and sycamore leaves and came out of the green canopy at unexpected angles.

One of Margaret's lyricists was Marnie, whose real name was Marcia Hersloff. My mother didn't know where her rival came from, thinking that she might belong to a Swedish shipping family, or that Carolyn's patron from the Cranbrook School might have introduced them, or that she might have come from out west. But one thing was definite: "She lived on an estate in Talbot County."

She was, in fact, the niece of Oliver Grymes, who had danced in Anna Pavlova's company under the stage name of André Olivéroff and had written a book about her, **Flight of the Swan: A Memory of Anna Pavlova.** *The copyright was renewed in 1960 by Marcia Grymes Hersloff, which was Marnie's full name.*

One of Carolyn's treasures was a pair of silver ankle bracelets, strings of little globes, each with a single rounded tip sticking out, that had belonged to Pavlova.

"Carrie, they look like bosoms!" my mother said one evening when they were showing me the ankle bracelets.

"Indeed they do," Carolyn answered, and they both laughed.

They really do resemble full breasts with prominent nipples—or at least they could serve as a kind of Rorschach test to see how sexually obsessed the subject in a psychological experiment might be. You can see the dents and hammer marks in each segment, the splices where the two halves of each globe join together, the minuscule palm fronds and florets on the armatures through which the chain links pass. They're also called ankle bells, and they jangle musically, a liquid gurgling, as you handle them. My mother deposited a note in a padded box that contains the bracelets. She wrote that they were "given to Carolyn Long by Oliver Grymes—dancer—Oxford, Md."

In the nursing home, my mother recalled that "a male dancer in Easton" had given the ankle bracelets to Carolyn. "He was queer," she said. "He had a boyfriend who was a dancer in the chorus of Pavlova." In fact, he himself was the dancer, and he had performed pas de deux with Pavlova, knowing "she would be easy to lift" but not expecting "the uncanny lightness of her."

In the press clippings my mother assembled, there's a newspaper photograph from the Easton **Star Democrat** of June 23, 1950, showing Carolyn standing on one side of a grand piano, sultry and gorgeous, looking seductively at the two songwriters who are holding the sheet music, Margaret smiling, Marnie looking serious, posing in the music room of Margaret's house, framed by frilly curtains around a pair of windows with half-open Venetian blinds.

The Arms of Morpheus

"Hearing is the last thing to go," the hospice nurse told me, "so talk to her. She'll be listening." It's easy to talk to the dead, who might be listening or not—like leaving a voice-mail message. The hard part is teaching the dead how to answer back.

In a life near its end, in a state of unconsciousness, the only activity of the day is a concentration on breathing and continuing to breathe. My mother, her pain eased by a constant flow of morphine, would have said, "I'm in the arms of Morpheus." She was already undergoing her metamorphosis, resting or gathering strength in a cocoon stage.

On Monday morning of her final week, when she was still conscious, my mother wanted to see her Siamese cat, after four months of saying "No, it'll make me sad," so I hurried back to my apartment and brought Aida to the nursing home. My mother opened her eyes, smiled when she saw Aida, and reached out for her. Soon after the cat settled on her lap, my mother drifted off. She had trouble breathing, and one of the nurses called her "unresponsive."

Three days earlier, before the weekend, my mother had coughed up blood. "She's requesting to go to heaven," an aide told me when I visited her near midnight. Her nose had been bleeding because it dried up from the oxygen, although the humidifier was bubbling, and the blood had apparently gone down her throat. I decided not to have her sent to the hospital.

On Saturday afternoon, I brought her grandchildren for a visit. She was propped up in bed, oxygen tubes in her nose, the bed-table laden with soft drinks, boxes of tissues, packets of crackers and candy (which she shared), and a coffee pot. She reminisced about going to junior high. "Mrs. Ross taught arithmetic," she said. "She loved the boys. She put me up at the blackboard. She called me a plum cup... a wrist box..."

"I remember that story," I said. "She called you a 'stuffed-up cream puff.'"

"I guess I didn't do it right. It was embarrassing."

She asked Eric and Becky what they were doing in school. She said she was sorry but she didn't feel up to playing Parcheesi or "Shut the Box," getting the name right after calling it, on previous visits, "Kick My Butt," "Skin the Cat," and "Knock the House Down." It made me wonder if she had been pulling my leg all along, acting as though she didn't remember things correctly, just to fool me.

When I mentioned what I'd been teaching in my classes at the university, she replied, "You're not the principal important subject of discussion."

Later, when I tried to call her, she didn't answer the phone because someone had put it on the bedside stand out of her reach, instead of leaving it on the portable table cantilevered over the bed. I saved her last phone message, which she had left on my voice mail sometime that weekend:

> *Just me. I don't know what's going to happen next. One of the girls came by, took my whole coffee pot that I had heated up and my nice, good Coke with ice and poured 'em down the sink. Honey, I haven't had a good day here. I love you, honey, bye.*

I wish I could go back and give her a Coca-Cola with ice, the way she offered refreshments to the letter carrier or the janitor or the delivery man from the drug store on a hot day. I wish I could make her day good. But remorse comes from what can't be changed, the permanence of certain mistakes and lapses. "It's never enough," I said to my mother when she expected more of me than I could supply, whenever she complained that I had "plenty of time for everybody else but me." She had a mother's gift for stirring up guilt.

On Sunday, I brought her a sausage biscuit, as I usually did every day. But she was asleep and didn't wake up while I was there. The following morning, I learned that she had tried to eat the biscuit but couldn't swallow anything. A nurse called to tell me that my mother was going on "continuous hospice care." I had read the booklet they gave me about "preparing for the end," so I knew she wouldn't live much longer. Dr. Bort, her final doctor, told me that her lungs had lost their elasticity.

And then, after smiling at Aida and reaching out to hold her, she slipped into in a deep sleep she couldn't be roused from. It reminded me of when she worked as a teller at the Bank of Bethesda and felt so tired at the end of the workday that she always took a nap before getting up to cook dinner and drink her "sody pops." Sometimes, though, she took sleeping pills and collapsed on her tester bed with the television on, and when I went in the room to turn off the set and check on her she looked dead. I tried to rouse her, pushing her shoulder, shoving harder and harder so her body rolled back and forth, saying, "Mom? Are you all right? Wake up, Mom, please." Then I'd listen for her breathing, which was very shallow, and leave the room when I heard it and saw the pulse on a vein of her neck, hoping she was all right but not sure what else I could do but let her sleep it off.

Now, she was really sleeping it off. Her breathing was always what worried me when she talked about her ailments. I felt sorry for her severe pain, usually at level ten when the doctor asked her to rate it, her misshapen, arthritic fingers, her hammer toes, her bad knees, her rotten teeth, her macular degeneration, her skin rashes and itchiness, her lack of appetite, and her trouble sleeping. But I knew that emphysema, her Chronic Obstructive Pulmonary Disease, would ultimately kill her.

Father David Howard, an Episcopal priest from Liberia, came into the room to minister to her needs. He had been talking with her about the Bible over the past couple of weeks, and the religious counsel had comforted her. Now, he intoned the "prayer for the sick," which he called her last rites. I remembered it from communion class as one of the sacraments, "extreme unction."

Many of the nurses and aides came in and told me how much they loved my mother, what a sweet lady she was: "She always said 'Where have you been?' when I came in and offered me candy—Milky Ways and Reese Cups. I'd say, 'I'm on a diet,' and she'd say, 'Have some. A little bit never hurt anyone.'" Another nurse said, "I blame your mother for the five pounds I've gained. Every time I came by she had that candy and she'd say, 'Dig in and take a handful.' She got mad if I said I couldn't."

Rebecca, an attentive, affectionate aide who had given my mother back rubs, cried and called her "my baby." An older aide named Jo said I was a wonderful son, a saint, but saints were just those who followed the Lord and were human.

On Tuesday, I cancelled my classes but attended my son Eric's high-school graduation that night. He was a piano major at the School for Creative and Performing Arts and had often played his pieces, such as Prokofiev's "Satanic Apparition," for my mother. I had wheeled her into the Black Box Theatre so she could hear him perform his own composition, "Dr. Snooks," with the jazz ensemble. Even the title had a connection with her life, named after the Persian cat her beloved sister Elizabeth left her when she died in a car crash. I took a video of Eric walking across the stage, hoping I could show it to my mother if she suddenly regained consciousness. The way he slouched across the stage reminded me of how my mother and Carolyn complained that I walked stoop-shouldered across the stage to receive my own diploma. "Shoulders back!" Carolyn used to bark at me. "Ramrod straight! Like a Marine standing at attention. Good posture is *crucial* if you ever want to cultivate a sense of well-being. You can't sing if you're stoop-shouldered."

My mother was breathing through her mouth, with the cannulae, the nostril pieces of her oxygen machine, lying on her tongue. She couldn't swallow, so liquid collected at the top of her throat and gurgled when she breathed.

While I was sitting by the bed, one of the nurses mentioned that I "popped in and out regularly." Another nurse told me, "She loved you to pieces. She said, 'I'm going to bust his butt if he writes that book. Then everyone will know all about me.'"

My mother, always opinionated, didn't like all of the nurses on her floor. But the ones she loved now gravitated to her bedside and lavished her with attention.

"Her body's shutting down," a drip-nurse named Chantee said, "but not all of the parts know that at the same time." She laughed about how my mother always wanted to eat dessert first. Angela, a hospice nurse who wore her hair in dreadlocks, added, "Whatever Miss Bobby wants, Miss Bobby gets."

Rebecca said, "She told it like it is, and I loved that about her. I'd lean over to her and whisper, 'You're my favorite, but don't tell anyone.'"

Angela recalled that "I'm tired" was the last thing she heard my mother say.

On Wednesday, her breathing was much slower, about 16 respirations per minute, as opposed to 37 the previous afternoon. She was lying with a damp cloth on her forehead, a green hospital gown covering her body, the stuffed kitty she had claimed was alive by her right hand, the nose piece positioned like a bit in a horse's mouth, her eyes almost closed. Foam padding, secured with Velcro, protected her feet and calves. Someone had applied them stylishly. They reminded me of go-go boots.

Outside the room, sitting in a wheelchair, a woman with short, straight white hair and a wide-eyed look was chanting "Oh God... Oh God," down a minor third from "Oh" to "God." Sometimes, though, it sounded like "All wrong... all wrong." Once, an old man using a walker passed by and imitated her, "Oh God, oh God."

My mother's hair was still iron gray, her wrists so thin they made her hands look large, smooth, quite beautiful. She had a striking profile, with her aristocratic nose and her distinguished, bristly, brushed-back hair. But her eyes were almost shut and her lashes very faint—because they were gray now, I realized.

Angela moistened my mother's mouth with Toothette swabs—rectangular green sponges on white lollipop sticks, dipped in water with a little lemon—and applied ChapStick to her lips. I asked, "Is she in a coma?"

Angela nodded but said, "We can't classify it as a coma because we'd need a brain scan. We call it a coma-like state."

On Thursday, my mother's hands looked blotchy, purplish, and her breathing was very fast, 50 respirations per minute. Her eyes were open. Angela told me that blood wasn't circulating to the extremities, so it was hard for her to get an oxygen level. When she finally got it, it registered 85, which was low.

"She'll go when she decides to go," she told me. "If she doesn't want you here, she'll wait until you go home."

Chantee, who wore rings on most of her fingers, administered concentrated morphine from a dropper, putting the tip under my mother's tongue, and then rubbed and stroked her neck. I looked out the open door to the corridor when I heard an aide say "Go fast! Nascar!" to aides who were pushing wheelchairs and another who was towing an oxygen machine. All of them wore blue smocks.

"Hearing is the last thing to go," I remembered, so I rubbed my mother's back and played music stations on the cable TV—Glenn Miller, the Andrews Sisters, opera arias, piano sonatas, anything that might make her happy if she could still hear it. And I talked to her, reminding her of everything that made her life matter: how wonderful, if often unappreciated, she had been as a mother; how lucky she and Carolyn had been to have a generous patron like Ruth; how devoted she had been to Carolyn; how courageous she had been about their love. I didn't talk about an afterlife but about the life before. I tried to go on and on as she would have done herself, and I thought of Wagner's idea of "continuous melody." I wanted my love song to be all aria, no recitative.

It was quiet, except for the gurgling of the humidifier, the humming and popping of the oxygen machine, the whirring of the fan, and some voices outside the door, including the woman who chanted "Oh, God... oh, God." My mother's breathing rate was 60 per minute. The stuffed kitty lay under her crossed hands. She wore a hospital gown with a pattern of thin, intersecting stripes. I observed what the booklet called "fish out of water" breathing, shallow gulps, her abdominal muscles moving.

By 4:00 p.m., her breaths were very shallow, although her heart was chugging along like the little engine that could. She let out a sigh. I was reminded of the opening stanza of John Donne's "A Valediction: Forbidding Mourning," which I had memorized when I was in the army:

> As virtuous men pass mildly away
> And whisper to their souls to go,
> While some of their sad friends do say
> The breath goes now, and some say No...

I looked closely at her lips, trying to tell if she was still taking any breaths. Sometimes there was a long interval before she sucked in a little air or released it. I felt ashamed that it reminded me of listening to popcorn in the microwave and counting the intervals between the kernels popping.

Her breathing just gradually stopped, her mouth moving less and less often, the pulse on her neck easing to a halt. There was a late breath, a sigh, and then nothing, but it was peaceful, an almost imperceptible drifting off. She died at 4:22 p.m. I checked my watch and wrote down the time on my legal pad. It was like the fade-out of a song, fainter and fainter until there was nothing but quietness. My mother looked comfortable until the end, cushioned by pillows, with folded-up sheets under her elbows.

And then her face started to turn yellow and waxy, as the doctor and nurses had told me it would. I remembered what my mother said about real pearls, how they turned yellow if you didn't wear them. Her cheeks and neck were becoming cool. Twenty minutes later, though, her back still felt warm as I rubbed it gently. She loved back rubs so much, it was hard to let go. And she was so terrified of being buried alive, I wanted to make sure she was really gone. I knew she would be zipped up in a plastic bag and transported to the funeral home, where she would be cremated. I also knew the cremation would not take place right away.

Nurses and aides came by, many of them weeping, paying their respects, saying their goodbyes. Rebecca, who was still calling my mother her baby, brought her daughter Jada. The aide my mother nicknamed Pearlie Mae said, "Miss Bobby, you're going to your mansion in heaven."

Around 5:00, a fire alarm went off. Nurses and aides rushed around, shutting doors while the alarm lights flashed and a harsh, pulsing sound buzzed. But I stayed where I was, and no one made any move to dislodge me from my mother's bedside. I turned off the oxygen machine and removed the cannulae from my mother's mouth. After it was clear that the nursing home was in no danger of burning, Angela came in, cleaned up my mother, and pulled a sheet over her head. From this point on, the nurses and aides were concerned about hiding the death from other patients.

A couple of male attendants slipped into the room and wheeled away my mother's covered body on a gurney. The patients stayed away from the corridor, almost like the frightened townspeople in *High Noon* who hide behind their curtains as Gary Cooper walks on the dusty street alone. I accompanied what remained of my mother, palpable enough that it wouldn't have startled me unpleasantly if she had reached out and clutched my wrist, the stereotypical shock of a horror movie that would have been welcome. When they reached the van that would take her to the funeral home, I said, "Goodbye, Mom, I love you," and let her go.

Disclosure #21

My mother often confided that when she dreamed about me, I was always nine years old. Eventually I realized that she was nine when she watched her father commit suicide in his rock garden. She claimed that she couldn't remember anything before then.

My first post-mortem dream about my mother happened a few nights after she died. Dressed in a gown tied in back, she lay on a gurney in a hospital room. The doctor told me he was going to operate next week, and I could be present, during surgery, if I wanted to hold her brains.

My mother was in good spirits but looked pale and felt tired. I crawled beside her on the gurney and cuddled. "Why, thank you," she said. "That's my boy."

Knick-knacks crowded the moveable bedside table. Yes, I was ready to hold her brains in my hands, like water cupped from a fountain, and let nothing spill. I would assist in the operation, and then I would ask my mother everything I had forgotten to ask, gathering her thoughts and recollections.

After I got up, left the room, and started to drive away, I thought, "Wait a minute. She was unconscious; she was in a coma. Then she got cremated. I've got to get back and see her while I've got the chance." But the roads went one way, and traffic was heavy, and I kept driving farther and farther in the opposite direction, trying to find a way to turn around, but I could never get back to the hospital parking lot.

Making Lists

"I wanted a spiral notebook," my mother said, "but I was shy, so Ebbie went into Woolworth's and asked for a 'spiritual notebook.'" She kept notebooks all her life, starting when she was a little girl, and devoted them primarily to lists. What prayers are to some people, lists were to Bobby. She recorded the minutiae of her life, and she was a close, shrewd observer. Had she been a voracious reader, she might have become a writer herself. She certainly took notes and gathered material in spiral notebooks, on yellow legal pads, on scraps of paper, on date books and calendars. The notebooks didn't look spiritual, but they were.

Starting when I was in elementary school, I walked to Safeway and did our grocery shopping, always supplied with a detailed list. The items often struck me as exotic—endives, chicory, sweetbreads, marzipan paste—but I was too shy to ask anyone who worked in the store for help, so I spent a lot of time searching through produce, canned goods, and refrigerated meat bins. Through the years, the lists kept coming, whether I lived with my mother, was visiting, or had an apartment nearby. She hated shopping, so she avoided doing it herself, preferring to hire boys from the neighborhood to deliver her groceries on their bikes.

She also made lists for errands she had to do or could delegate to someone else. When I talked with her on the phone, I could always tell if she was working through a list as we talked. She listed the coins in her collection, cars she had owned, cats she had adopted, medications she was taking, and medical crises she had endured, including a bout with tuberculosis that had confined her to a sanatorium for several weeks when she was a teenager.

After my mother died, I looked carefully, piece by piece, through a brown binder I had taken away from her apartment before she could prevent me from removing it and possibly destroy the evidence she had gathered about herself. She made a faint objection, saying, "No, Johnny, don't bother with that now," but she was propped up on a ramp of pillows, oxygen cannulae in her nostrils, the poster advertising Carolyn's appearance on "Harvest of Stars" above her bed, and she was in no position to leap up and try to wrestle the binder away from me. The most surprising item was a list on a lined sheet ripped from a spiral notebook:

1961-1975 (14 years)

1	1	Larry	@ 1961 (4857)
sev	2	Bob Ewald	1968-70 (4903)

sev	3	John Bowman	1968-70 (4903)
1	4	Andy	1969 (4903)
2	5	taxi man New Years Eve (baker by day)	@ 1966 (4903)
1	6	man @ Sibley Hosp.	1963 (5145)
1	7	Dr. Peterson, dentist	1960s (Rehoboth)
1	8	Karl Neflin	1969 (4903)
1	9	Frank Carper	1974 (4909 #101)
1	10	"Sammie"	1975 (4909 #102)
1	11	Male Beautician on Arlington Rd.	1961 (4857)

<u>NO</u>
1 Cashell
2 George Le.C.
3 Tom Spon
4 Otis
5 Sky Jackson
6 liquor store guy on Wisc. Av
7 Fritz Gerdes proposition

Several lines down, one entry stood by itself:

CL [Carolyn Long]
1958-1968

The dates look like engravings on tombstones. I recognized immediately what I had found: her list of sexual encounters with men during the time she and Carolyn were a couple. And I was shocked, sorry I hadn't examined the paper before she died so I could interrogate her about it. I was fine about her sexual relationship with Carolyn, their commitment to each other, the affection they shared. I was not fine about a series of promiscuous one-afternoon stands with men, many of whom I had actually met, including one of her high-school boyfriends (Larry), a pair of young co-workers at the bank (John and Frank), an auto mechanic (Bob), a car salesman (Andy), and even one of Carolyn's voice students (Karl).

I knew about only one of those sexual episodes first-hand. On New Year's Eve at the end of 1966, I went on a double date. The girl who was going with my friend Mike felt sick, so we dropped her off early, and I returned to our apartment's parking lot to drop off Mike, who was staying with us because his parents were diplomats stationed in Africa and he attended St. Albans School and had nowhere else to go. I wanted to find a secluded spot to make out with Nancy, who had written "1967" on part of the windshield that was fogged up, but Mike made a sad face and complained that he'd be lonely. Nancy wanted him to come along, so I relented, but I was a bad sport about it, sulking while Mike leaned over the front seat between us. Nancy gave me the briefest kiss when I dropped her off at her front door.

When we got back to the apartment, my mother and a strange man, both obviously drunk, were standing in the living room. She introduced him as the man who drove her home in his taxi after she left a party. He went away, but I was in the kitchen when he came back with a white sack from People's Drug Store. In bed, I couldn't sleep because I was so upset and jealous about Nancy's flirting with Mike. I became embarrassed when I heard grunting noises coming from my mother's room next door. I realized that the taxi driver must have gone out for condoms. In the morning, my mother, who was hung over, made a shy apology, saying, "I'm sorry I wasn't myself. It was New Year's Eve, and I wanted to celebrate."

She never mentioned sex, but I knew what she meant. That was probably the lowest point in my mother's life with Carolyn. We had moved out of the beautiful house on Massachusetts Avenue a few months before then, and Carolyn was living alone in the District of Columbia. My mother had precipitated the break-up, and I imagined that the heterosexual sex was partly to get back at Carolyn and partly to convince herself she wasn't really a lesbian. But it felt wrong to me, a betrayal of Carolyn, whom I thought of as a surrogate parent.

Based on my personal knowledge of this encounter with the taxi driver, I realized that the list enumerated men with whom she had had intercourse over a period of 14 years, almost all of it when she was involved, if not actually living, with Carolyn. The first number must have indicated how many times they had "done it," usually just once. The "2" in front of the unnamed taxi driver, who also worked as a baker, probably meant they had sex once before Mike and I got home and once after. Two men had "sev," or "several times," before their names. My mother even noted the dates and the places of these assignations, 4857 indicating the Glenwood apartment on Battery Lane, 5145 our house on Massachusetts Avenue, 4903 the apartment on Battery Lane after my mother and I left the house, 4909 (#101) the one-bedroom apartment above Carolyn's studio, and 4909 (#102) the three-bedroom apartment the two women shared. The list reeks of revenge.

The column labeled "NO" included men who pursued my mother but were spurned. Cashell Shoemaker was her predecessor as head teller at the main branch of the Bank of Bethesda. "I never did anything with him," my mother said, "but people sure liked to talk about us. You know how people gossip."

"You led him on," I told her. "He was always running errands for you, picking you up, bringing you presents."

"Yes," she said, "he was one of my lackeys. I can't help it if he had a case on me."

Cashell acted as foolishly as the professor in *Der blaue Engel* who debased himself because of his infatuation with Marlene Dietrich. His puppyish devotion to my mother was embarrassing, especially since he was white-haired and retired, like Uncle Guy but without the money. He claimed to have one of my mother's pubic hairs, which he found on our toilet seat, in his wallet, along with one from his wife, Goldie, a Kindergarten teacher who once said "Now what do Bobby and Cashell know that Goldie doesn't know?" The funny thing is, that pubic hair in his personal shrine might very well have been mine, since I used the same bathroom.

Otis Williams, another man whose advances my mother repelled while accepting his gifts, was a big, fat, bald man who sold real estate and had a lot of money. When he came to our apartment for dinner, he brought Delmonico steaks my mother cooked for the three of us. He liked to go the race track, took my mother several times, and placed a two-dollar bet for me on a horse named Greek Money that later went on to win the Preakness. (I made $13, which he gave to my mother so she could pass it along to me.) After he died, when my mother was broke, she used to say, "I should have married Otis. He was sweet. Never asked for anything, except a good-night kiss." I don't think she ever said she should have married Uncle Guy, who was much richer than Otis.

I think my mother was reminding herself that she was choosy, not available to all comers, but it looks like capriciousness. I remember how, in the Sixties, she used to go downtown in the District of Columbia with her friend Alberta. They would pick up a couple of men and have a few rounds of cocktails, but then my mother would fabricate some excuse and take a taxi home. Her bolting made Alberta furious. At the very least, my mother was ambivalent about relations with men.

I was sad and surprised to realize that my mother's sex life with Carolyn may have ended in 1968, when she was 44 and Carolyn was 53. But physical intimacy involved more than an exchange of orgasms, and I know they continued to sleep together, at least on occasion, until they moved out of their three-bedroom apartment in Bethesda and Carolyn entered the Mallard Bay nursing home in Cambridge.

The list of affairs was a matter of setting the record straight. But it was also a way to test and guide her memory, to recover the past, however embarrassing.

Disclosure #22

The most obsessive list-making my mother indulged in—not counting grocery lists, which were pragmatic—involved recording the names of friends and relatives who had died. She kept redoing those lists, putting the names in address books or pocket calendars or spiral notebooks, the way I kept recalculating the number of days I had left in my tour of duty when I was serving in the army. After most of the names, she jotted down dates, but after some there were question marks. She left multiple copies of these necrologies. It was a way of saying "I am alive, I have survived," as well as declaring "I remember."

She was paying tribute, performing a ritual she hoped people would perform in her memory. It was a way to embrace not only those lost friends, even if some were really acquaintances who wouldn't remember her, but also her own life, to lay claim on her connections and choices.

My mother could expiate her guilt at not keeping in touch with Fran Pflug, an awkward spinster who worked with her at the bank and accompanied us once on a trip to Ocean City, by writing down her name and thinking about their experiences together. In concentrated form, those catalogues of the dead made up her own memoir.

Varieties of Religious Experience

My mother's true religion was superstition. Whenever she asked for salt at the dinner table, she would not accept the shaker if someone picked it up and extended it to her. She insisted that it be placed on the table. "It's bad luck to hand it over directly," she explained by way of apology.

She dispensed superstitions as practical advice: always leave by the same door where you came in; throw a pinch of salt over your shoulder when you spill some; don't walk under ladders; whenever you see a truck with a load of hay, make a wish, but don't look back or the wish will not come true. There was always a good deal of knocking on wood in our household, and if we were riding in the car it was a matter of knocking on vinyl—anything to ward off a jinx.

She taught me that it was good luck, on the first day of every month, to say "Rabbit" as soon as you woke up. I'm not sure why that should be the magic word, but forgetting to utter it, the way other people might say grace before a meal or prayers before bed, would strike me even now as a desecration of her memory. She observed her rituals faithfully. And religion itself was one of her superstitions.

My mother liked to recount the story that she was baptized in water from the River Jordan. "Mrs. Dick brought back several bottles and gave some to Mother," she said. "When they opened it in Christ Church it smelled so bad it almost killed them. But it meant a lot to me." She wasn't, however, much of a churchgoer, at least not after we left Cambridge. When I was a boy soprano at St. John's Episcopal Church in Bethesda, she dropped me off for choir rehearsal on Sunday morning and for evensong later in the day, but she didn't usually attend the services herself. She followed Emily Dickinson's alternative of keeping the Sabbath by "staying at home." It was her day to "un-lax." She couldn't bear how the minister's sermons always ended with an appeal for more money in the collection plates. When she did go to services, she was primarily concerned about having a hat to wear, and if she didn't have something to cover her head, she pulled out a handkerchief (or even a piece of Kleenex), unfolded it, and used a bobby-pin to secure it to her hair. It sounds like superstition.

In *The Varieties of Religious Experience*, William James observes that religious experience "spontaneously and inevitably engenders myths, superstitions, dogmas, creeds, and metaphysical theologies, and criticisms of one set of these by the adherents of another." The whole list, not just "superstitions," applied to my mother, who was bound by tradition but also an escape artist who wriggled out of those slippery chains whenever the mood struck.

She had an iconoclast's aversion to the trappings of religion, another aspect of her rebellious streak. She wasn't used to incense or genuflection, and somehow her indignation made her sacrilegious. After she underwent surgery at Georgetown University Hospital and came out of anesthesia, she rang for a nurse, who turned out to be a nun. She pointed at the wall and demanded, "Take down that crucifix." The sight of Jesus writhing on the cross gave her the creeps. "Seeing that all day long," she explained, "wouldn't help my recovery."

At a wedding in Washington, when I was a teenager, she nudged her friend Fredericka and asked, "What's that thing up there?" She pointed toward a gold vessel called the tabernacle, the repository for the Eucharist.

"Shh!" Fred whispered. "God's in there."

"Ooh," my mother said, "He must be such a little man!"

Her own mother, Sadie, called the Bible "the dirtiest book ever written," and I don't recall my mother spending any time reading scripture. But that may be because she felt those matters were private, not public. When I went through a born-again phase as a teenager, my mother looked very uncomfortable if I made declarations of faith. I might as well have been extolling Communism.

But she did invest time in religious study as she grew more afraid of dying. After she started to watch Reverend Schuller preaching in the Crystal Cathedral on television, inspirational magnets, with inscriptions like "Inch by inch, anything's a cinch," appeared on her refrigerator. In a pocket notebook, she wrote down quotations from Billy Graham. She had seen him once on a train, walking through the dining car, and told me, "He was so handsome, so tall, the kind of man who makes my toes curl." Faith required beauty.

My mother's urn was screwed shut when I picked it up from the funeral home. Later, I wished I had opened it and poured some of her remains into the cloisonné jar she had joked about using as the receptacle for her ashes when she died. Whenever I look at the jar now, I'm saddened by the vacancy, although I don't imagine that a portion of her ashes would lessen the grief or offer any consolation.

My mother's memorial service, just like Carolyn's sixteen years before, took place by the marker the two women shared, under a tent with the sides open, with two dozen folding chairs and an altar holding her urn and the framed photographs I had supplied. One showed my mother as a Southern Belle in the rock garden where her father had killed himself.

The minister came from a Methodist church in Madison, the village where Sadie was born, in the marshy land by the Chesapeake Bay, and emphatically not from Christ Church, where she had been baptized and where her ancestors were buried in the graveyard. It struck me as a final act of rebellion. Wearing a green robe, he stressed that our material bodies were temporary but our spirits were eternal, going on and on about my mother's "material existence," asserting that it wasn't all-important. In heaven, he said, "we'll be able to perfect ourselves and the things we've tried to do." He claimed that my mother would have time in heaven to perfect how she played the piano.

When it was my turn to share some memories of Bobby, I talked about how my mother kept her fiery spirit until the end, refusing to go to dinner with the other patients because she didn't want to be around old people. I told everyone about how my mother once made me promise to put Aida, her Siamese cat, to sleep when she died and to mingle their ashes. "I'm glad to tell you," I said, "that Aida is not in the urn. My mother knew how well I was taking care of her cat and released me from the promise—which I wouldn't have kept anyway."

Although I didn't have Aida put to sleep when my mother died, I still intended to bring the cat's remains to the graveyard eventually, dig a hole near the marker, and deposit the ashes. My mother rejected the idea of a heaven that didn't include cats. She was indignant that anyone or any religion could dispute the fact that Aida had a soul.

Back in the three-bedroom apartment when Carolyn, already disabled and suffering from all sorts of medical problems, had an attack of what my second ex-wife called "some fake disease," they summoned an Episcopal priest to administer the last rites. He asked if Carolyn had been baptized. They said yes, embarrassed to admit the truth.

I was living in New York when my mother phoned and announced, "Carolyn was baptized last night, right here in our own apartment. Isn't that wonderful? Does it still count if it wasn't a priest who did it?"

"Yes," I said, "it's the spirit that matters, not what denomination the person who performed the ceremony might belong to."

"Does it have to be a person?"

"What do you mean?"

"We had Tippi do it."

"You mean the cat?"

"We were drinking. We were worried because Carolyn almost died recently and was never baptized. We boiled water to make it holy, let it cool off, and dipped Tippi's paw in and rubbed it in the shape of a cross on Carrie's forehead. I recited something from the Book of Common Prayer."

Once they were back in Cambridge, my mother made sure that Carolyn had a real baptism, with Reverend Whatley presiding, the ceremony taking place on my mother's birthday. There were two godmothers: Ruth Small, Carolyn's patron and former classmate, and Nancy Fleming, who had worked as one of my mother's maids when I was a boy and now served as one of Carolyn's care-givers. Appropriately enough, there was no godfather.

Aida outlived my mother by half a year. She was 16, suffering because her bowels wouldn't move and the "stool," as the doctor called it, had become impacted, so I took her to the vet's office to have her put to sleep. She sat on my lap as I drove, and I held her as the doctor stuck in the needle that euthanized her. Later, I donated the framed painting of Aida to the veterinary clinic, where it now hangs in the corridor to the examination rooms.

I returned to the Eastern Shore on a research trip in October 2009, but my first order of business was to reunite my mother and her cat. It was nearly dark when I checked into the Day's Inn on Route 50 and drove to Dorchester Memorial Park, stopping on the gravel lane near the plot my mother and Carolyn shared. After unlocking the trunk of my car, I opened a wooden box, removed the plastic bag containing Aida's ashes from a velvet drawstring pouch, and picked up the garden trowel I had brought for the reverse grave-robbing I was about to undertake. I imagined it was illegal to deposit a pet's remains in a cemetery, but I felt compelled to honor my mother's wishes. Still, I looked around nervously and listened. No one was lurking in the vicinity.

I said hello to Carolyn when I walked around her side of the marker and then knelt by my mother's side and plunged the trowel into the grass a few inches from the granite. I figured that I couldn't possibly go as deep as my mother's urn. I dug up a divot and removed it carefully, figuring I could put it back on top like a toupee on the bald mound of dirt mixed with Aida's "cremains." I snipped the plastic bag with scissors I pulled from my pocket and dumped the ashes into the hole, but it was more than I expected, and I had the sudden fear that I had failed to dig deep enough and would be caught. I stirred white ashes and dark earth together, but there was too much for the available space, so I sprinkled some of the mixture on the nearby grass and replaced the divot of turf, packing it down, pressing with the side of the trowel, trying to make everything fit and lie relatively flat. When I was done, there was a red glow in the west, and headlights zipped by on the highway. It was hard to see anything, since night had just about fallen, but I thought I could still detect the off-white grains of ashes among the close-cropped blades of the lawn. Still kneeling, I said some words to my mother, telling her how I missed her every day, how I wished I could talk with her, and how Aida was with her now.

The tombstone was a declaration of love, a defiant gesture at everyone and everything that had thwarted my mother in her life. She was resting at peace with both her true love, Carolyn, and her one-person cat, Aida. I was happy that any casual visitor to the cemetery could probably read their story in the monument itself. My mother wore it like Hester Prynne's scarlet letter that was reproduced on *her* gravestone. Carolyn Long may have lost her nerve about singing, but my mother never lost her nerve about Carolyn, no matter how much she wavered.

When she instructed the engraver to put their names on opposite sides of the tombstone, she had no idea that their marker would emulate the one shared by Gertrude Stein and Alice B. Toklas in Père Lachaise Cemetery in Paris. But the connection makes sense beyond the bond of sexual proclivities—and beyond the opera libretti Stein wrote for Virgil Thomson, who had reviewed one of Carolyn's performances in *Jeanne d'Arc au bûcher.* I often played a recording of Gertrude Stein reciting her Cubist portrait of Picasso, "If I told him would he like it, would he like it if I told him," with the idea that the repetitions would drive my mother a little crazy. It became a game between us, and she was fond of the ritualized, literary teasing, although she did confuse Gertrude Stein with Edith Sitwell. It was characteristic of her that she mixed up names. Once, when I was suffering from poison ivy, she was getting ready to drive to Brentano's Book Store and asked if she could buy me anything. I asked for a book of poems by George Herbert. When she came home, she told me she was sorry, but they didn't have anything by George Victor. It turned out that she had used the name of the operetta composer Victor Herbert as a mnemonic device.

I used to joke that we should put a bass clef on my mother's side of the tombstone to go with Carolyn's treble clef, along with the title of another Verdi aria, "Celeste Aida," both to match Carolyn's "Pace, Pace, Mio Dio" and to hint at the secret interment, then merely conjectural, of her Siamese cat. But of course, my mother was not a professional musician, so any musical symbol would seem presumptuous. And even if one appeared, it would really have to be a matching treble clef, since they were both women. What really belonged on her side was the Biblical phrase "Whither Thou Goest," since my mother had forsaken the generations of her own family in the Christ Church graveyard for the company of Carolyn's family, the Creightons, out in the country near a stand of crepe myrtles and Route 50.

My mother had pretended to be conventional to ward off being controversial. It didn't fool most people, who clearly had their suspicions. More and more, people had thought of her as a "character." Her outrageous comments could deflect how outrageous she truly was. She was defensive about her relationship with Carolyn and said, about a prying neighbor, "She accused me of being queer. I told her, 'No, Carolyn is my dearest friend.'" They were a couple, and it didn't matter how they qualified the public cover story of their private union. She denied what they were, the love they shared, but she was not in denial.

Part of her wanted to be a rebel and be outrageous, but part of her wanted to be a good girl. She was scared of so much, especially running out of money. She had a religious side that came partly from tradition, partly from a yearning to lead a "normal" life, partly from a fear of death, and partly from the hope of reconciling herself to the way she had chosen to lead her life.

Over her last few years, my mother and I spent a lot of time discussing whether there was any life after death. I quoted Robert Frost's "Birches": "Earth's the right place for love: / I don't know where it's likely to go better." She entertained Gore Vidal's notion that human beings might be nothing more than viruses. But she retreated into the comfort rendered by the concept of the hereafter. "You just like to argue," she said. "You'll feel different when you're my age."

Logic could not discourage her hopeful thinking, her anxious faith, her superstitions. At the end, I think she did believe. She loved Carolyn much too much to deny the possibility of an afterlife, the chance for a reunion. She could not bear the thought that they might not see each other again. But she also expected her cat to join them.

Disclosure #23

I invited my father to attend Bobby's memorial service—which seemed like a possibility, since he had taken a couple of trips with his beautiful 80-year-old girlfriend (a native of Switzerland who still spoke with a charming French accent) to nearby St. Michael's—but he declined. He was still, after all, the odd man out in that threesome from the Fifties. My mother had wanted to outlive him so she could collect the $19,000 life insurance policy he was required, by their divorce agreement, to maintain with her as the beneficiary. But the difference in their longevity may have been caused by her continuing to smoke long after he had quit.

After my stepmother Cornelia died in January 2006, her longtime friend Chantal phoned my father to ask how he was doing. "I don't want to live much longer," he told her. "There's no point. I hate using a cane. I'm depressed. All I want to do is eat, so going out to a restaurant is the highlight of my day."

She invited him to lunch on his birthday in June because he seemed lost after Cornelia was gone. "But then there was a spark," she told me, "and he seemed to come alive again, and he told me he loved me. Your father made me feel grounded."

In a jubilant phone call, my father claimed it was the first time he had ever fallen in love. He wanted to marry Chantal, but she refused. "I need my independence," she declared. "I need my space." And she refused to let him stay at her apartment in Jackson Heights more than three nights a week. But he still called her his "common-law wife."

My father lost a number of longtime friends when he fell madly in love with her. A husband and wife, both professional singers, were shocked when he started dating six months after Cornelia died. "He was all enthusiastic about the new woman in his life," Chantal said, "and they couldn't take it, couldn't accept it. But what's a man supposed to do? Stop living?"

Chantal told me that she and my father were "like a couple of teenagers." Her late husband didn't want any silliness (and neither did Cornelia), but the two of them "let loose together." She liked to come up from behind and touch his neck or his arms, and he said, "Ooh, no one ever did that before."

I phoned my father every day after Cornelia's death, but he never talked openly about why he went away. He was moved, though, to tell Chantal his side of the story. When he left our house on Labor Day Weekend, he took nothing, just the clothes he was wearing. He returned the car, leaving it in Wilmington, and took the train back to New York. Things were tight. When he got his first paycheck, he had one dollar in his wallet. He worked three jobs: at Barney's, in a bank, and singing in a choir. He shared an apartment with a roommate—cheaper than living on his own.

He confided to her why he had left my mother and me: "I couldn't take it anymore. I had to get out. We were married, but it didn't feel like it. We were strangers. I was working two jobs and away a lot. When I came back one time..." The trailing off was suggestive, but he didn't elaborate on the sordid details. He said that my mother was more interested in another woman and gave all her attention to her friend. Finally, when he "couldn't take it anymore," he left, but he gave her the car and the house. He was worried that he had been a bad father. "But fathers didn't have much to do with bringing up their children then," Chantal said. "He did the best he could. He loved you very much. 'Why don't you tell him?' I asked, but he couldn't." My father didn't think I really missed him, since I had made my own life, but Chantal thought he didn't realize how much he had hurt me and "at what cost."

Full Moon on the Water

On July 31, 1958, the moon had just passed the point of being completely full, but it would have still looked full to my mother and Carolyn as they drove the Chevrolet Bel-Air from the gravel parking lot of Whispering Pines, strewn with brown needles, where they had just bought a fifth of bourbon, and eased down the single-lane Buck Bryan Road, with loblolly pines on one side and corn fields on the other. The road was named for the owner of the liquor store and led to his house on the shore of Bolingbroke Creek, which everybody called Bowling Brook.

Their windows would have been wide open, since cars didn't have air-conditioning in those days and it was a warm, humid summer night. But a breeze was blowing off the water. The question was, did they pull into the woods in one of the clearings or did they continue toward the water? How do I know, in any case, what they were doing on that particular night?

My mother liked to keep records. I learned from her how to annotate receipts when I paid bills, but only when she was too ill to do her own and I had to take over. Once you start the habit, if you're the slightest bit obsessive-compulsive, you have to continue, if only for the "tiny insane voluptuousness" that Theodor Storm describes in his poem about working at a desk, the pleasure of completing tasks, finally getting things done.

She liked to keep a date book for each year, so I have a record of when she did this and did that. On July 31, she almost always remembered to write "CBD and CL" and "Anniversary" and however many years had passed since 1958. What were they celebrating? Why did my mother continue to commemorate the date?

I didn't know the answer until my mother died, when I went through a large plastic storage box she kept under her bed. I knew she had destroyed a stack of letters Carolyn had received, presumably from lovelorn suitors whom she had spurned. She claimed she had burned them, but that sounds like a lot of work and a sooty mess if you lacked a fireplace. She made a point of telling me that she disposed of the letters so I wouldn't get them and use them as "material."

But she did not get rid of Carolyn's green diary for 1958, the crucial year that was both *annus mirabilis* and *annus horribilis* for the two women and me. My mother kept it in a tin box, among her dearest treasures. Although the book said "Diary," it was really a date-book like those my mother kept, except more elegantly bound. Carolyn had marked down reminders about which students had voice lessons when, which friends she was seeing for dinner, whose birthdays were coming up, which doctors' appointments she had to keep. Every month, she wrote "CURSE" in red letters, presumably to indicate her menstrual periods. On December 18, she wrote "We Started South" when the three of us left Maryland and headed toward Texas, not knowing then that we wouldn't get past Alabama.

Here's what she wrote in her diary on July 31, with the date underlined:

> *Marito*
> *e moglie*
> *felice per sempre*

"Husband and wife, happy forever." And then I knew how to put things together. My mother and Carolyn had exchanged vows, under a full moon, either inside or outside the car, near the water and the pines, by a side road where no cars disturbed them. My mother had told me she always liked necking better than sex and had declared that no one gave better back rubs than Carolyn, so exquisite that she threatened to cut off Carolyn's fingers and keep them after she died, no matter how grotesque that sounded. Part of it may have been hero worship, a fan's adoration, a schoolgirl crush, but she was smitten—both of them were.

Thinking about this privileged moment, this peak of intimacy, this private, secret, do-it-yourself wedding in the woods by the water, I imagined a motion-picture camera pulling back discreetly from the Chevy and slowly panning down the road between pines and cornfields, surging toward the creek and the Choptank River in the distance, settling on the rippling full moon on the water, accompanied by the sound of clanking bell-buoys, the slosh of waves, the low buzz of a johnboat trolling in the dark, a gull or a mallard ruffling its feathers and taking flight. And then, from the car, the sound of "Whither Thou Goest," a hit song by Les Paul and Mary Ford, would emerge from the radio, with Carolyn singing along, the lyrics quoting from the Bible: "Whither thou goest, I will go." My mother, the former Sunday School teacher, surely knew the passage from the Book of Ruth:

> Intreat me not to leave thee, or to return from following after thee: for whither thou goest, I will go; and where thou lodgest, I will lodge: thy people shall be my people, and thy God my God:
> Where thou diest, will I die, and there will I be buried: the Lord do so to me, and more also, if ought but death part thee and me.

Before I actually read that lovely book from the Old Testament, I came upon "Ruth and Naomi," a poem by Edward Field in *Stand Up, Friend, with Me*, the first poetry collection I was ever given, in which he describes how "Ruth and Naomi, lip to vaginal lip, / Proclaimed their love throughout the land." Of course, I didn't see any personal connection until much later, after I had started writing my own poems, had read more poetry, and had learned more about my mother and Carolyn, especially how to empathize with the predicament they faced every day: hiding and denying their intimate relationship, a love that deserved celebration, not concealment.

Among my mother's loose papers, the phrase "Whither Thou Goest" appears repeatedly, without explanation. But the words were a pledge, a promise that wherever one of them went the other would follow, and despite the social pressure against their union and the combustible nature of their personalities they would honor that contract which no one had witnessed, my mother not abandoning Carolyn in her final illness but tending to her needs, more devoted than any cousin could be, and ultimately following her to the grave plot they shared, with their names on opposite sides of the granite marker, taking her place next to Carolyn's parents, forsaking her own family and declaring her love in the most permanent way she could. I'm pretty sure that Carolyn sang the words of the popular song and that my mother, her most devoted fan, responded both to the seductive music and the soothing religion it encapsulated. And the romantic, moonlit night by the woods and the water was an essential part of that makeshift, spontaneous, what-the-hell ceremony that bound them so tightly together. They were giving all to love.

Carolyn's green diary also contained a note for my mother that she had composed in shaky script on a small sheet of paper. It served as a bookmarker for the page that celebrated their marriage to each other. It may have been the last thing she was able to write:

>My darling I love you
>beyond all measure
>There is no separation
>All I know is
>I love you more
>than I ever could
>believe. It is a love
>that knows no end
>Love me
>Love me endlessly
>I will wait
>   Your Carrie

During one of the last nights she spent in her own apartment, before entering the Western Hills nursing home, my mother was surprised when

I seized that binder of notes about her life and said I was taking it home for safe-keeping. I was afraid she would destroy those personal reminders, which included several references to "Buck Bryan Road" and "Whither Thou Goest," those fragments toward an autobiography she could never manage to begin, just as she had destroyed the trove of Carolyn's correspondence. She objected a little but then relented. She knew I was planning to write about her. "I just worry," she said, "that we started too late and I won't be able to tell you all my stories, all my secrets." But the point wasn't to be encyclopedic.

"That's okay," I told her. "We have enough."

*   *   *

Acknowledgments

Several chapters and *Disclosures* first appeared in literary magazines: "The House That She Designed" in *The Gettysburg Review* (Summer 2011); "My Mother's Choice" in *Alligator Juniper* (May 2017); "Full Moon on the Water" in *Delmarva Review* (November 2022); "Fishing Pier and Hunting Lodge," "*Disclosure #9*" (under the title "Disclosure about My Mother"), and "*Disclosure #21*" (under the title "First Dream of My Mother after Her Death") in *Live Encounters Poetry & Writing* (December 2022). I want to thank the editors of these journals—Peter Stitt; Sheila Sanderson; Ellen Brown and Wilson Wyatt; and Mark Ulyseas—for accepting and publishing them.

Two poems from my first full-length collection, *The Disappearing Town* (Miami University Press, 2000), are reprinted in this memoir: "Storm on Fishing Bay" (originally published in *Western Humanities Review*, Fall 1993, and now retitled "Storm Approaching") and "Soprano" (*The Antioch Review*, Summer 1983). I'm grateful to the editors who accepted them: James Reiss, Richard Howard, and David St. John.

A travel grant from the Charles Phelps Taft Foundation allowed me to return to Cambridge, Maryland, and conduct interviews. A sabbatical from the English Department at the University of Cincinnati gave me time to start and write about half of this book.

In writing and revising this memoir, I've depended on spoken remarks recorded in journals and pocket notebooks, quotations from letters, interviews with people my mother and her partner Carolyn knew, as well as my own memories of exactly what people said and resaid. Although I have had to reconstruct some dialogue, I haven't fabricated any conversations that didn't actually take place.

I'm indebted to many people who contributed to this memoir, but I could not have made much progress without the archives my mother kept. The notes, diaries, date books, letters, photographs, clippings, scrapbooks, and other memorabilia helped enormously. So did the history of our family she compiled and the two thick volumes of Carolyn Long's press clippings she assembled: her "two literary accomplishments." I am thankful for how fully and frankly she answered the many nosy questions I posed in the last months of her life, when she knew that I was planning to write a book about her experiences with Carolyn. I just wish that I could still talk with her.

I would like to thank Dail Mahood Richie, John and Jean Walker, Sherry Small Sundick, Bob Kirwan, Susan Wingate, and several people who are no longer alive (Earl Brannock, Atwood Henry, Larry Henry, and Frank Wright) for sharing their recollections of my mother and Carolyn. Chantal Wiegner let me know about things my father had revealed to her but was unable to divulge to me.

My friend and colleague Michael Griffith read a draft of the whole memoir and offered invaluable suggestions and welcome encouragement. Jillian Weise gave me helpful, generous comments on the manuscript. Michael Martone served as a university press's reader of an earlier version, and the press sent me a copy of his review that had recommended it for publication.

Barbara Smith-Mandell advised me about how to tighten up the manuscript and accepted an earlier version of the memoir for Truman State University Press, but they couldn't publish it because they lost their funding from the state of Missouri and went out of business.

I have worked on this memoir for many years, revising and rearranging the chapters, cutting the manuscript from a high of 98,000 words to the current 60,000. I found some of the rejections I received generous in their encouragement, regrets, and advice (even when it provoked me into going in the opposite direction), and I want to thank the following agents and editors: Eleanor Jackson, Caryn Karmatz Rudy, Chris Parris-Lamb, and Maria Massie; Gary Kass (Acquisitions Editor of the University of Missouri Press), Mary Azrael and Kendra Kopelke (Editors of Passager Books), Barrett Warner (Book Acquisitions Editor of Galileo Press), Larry Moore (Editor of Broadstone Books), and Ron Sauder (Editor of Secant Publishing).

I am infinitely grateful to the editors of Finishing Line Press—Leah Huete de Maines, Kevin Maines, and Christen Kincaid—for accepting this memoir and guiding it into publication.

My wife, LaWanda Walters, got me going with the actual composition of this book when I was bogged down in research, encouraging me to avoid email and the web, put my notes aside, and simply write. She was generous with her keen insights and editorial suggestions both global and local. I am especially grateful for how she convinced me to delete chapters that were not contributing to the main themes and narrative arc. Her incisive criticism was crucial to this memoir.

John Philip Drury is the author of six collections of poetry: *The Stray Ghost* (a chapbook-length sequence from State Street Press, 1987), *The Disappearing Town* (Miami University Press, 2000), *Burning the Aspern Papers* (Miami University Press, 2003), *The Refugee Camp* (Turning Point Books, 2011), *Sea Level Rising* (Able Muse Press, 2015), and *The Teller's Cage: Poems and Imaginary Movies* (Able Muse Press, 2024). He has also written *Creating Poetry* and *The Poetry Dictionary*, both from Writer's Digest Books. His awards include an Ingram Merrill Foundation fellowship, two Ohio Arts Council grants, a Pushcart Prize, and the Bernard F. Conners Prize from *The Paris Review*. He was born in Cambridge, Maryland, and grew up in Bethesda, raised by his mother and a former opera singer. After dropping out of college and losing his draft deferment during the Vietnam War, he enlisted in the army and served undercover at the West German Refugee Camp near Nuremberg. He used benefits from the G.I. Bill to earn degrees from Stony Brook University, the Writing Seminars at Johns Hopkins, and the Iowa Writers' Workshop. After teaching at the University of Cincinnati for 37 years, he is now an emeritus professor and lives with his wife, fellow poet LaWanda Walters, in a hundred-year-old house on the edge of a wooded ravine.